Is That Really in the Bible?

Cletus McMurtry

ISBN: 979-8-89228-863-7   (Paperback)
ISBN: 979-8-89228-864-4   (Hardcover)
ISBN: 979-8-89228-865-1   (eBook)

Printed in the United States of America

Contents

To my wife, Melanie Bean McMurtry, for her abiding love, understanding, and encouraging wisdom.

Preface

Why is it that when you ask two Bible experts about the same biblical contents, you may get three different answers? Maybe it's time to look at the Bible form a non-expert view. A person just like you, that was shown discrepancies between what used to be written and what is now written in the new Bibles. If that scares you, it should. Think about it.

Introduction

We are not going to talk about religion. Instead, we are going to examine and discuss the Holy Bible in a way unlike any you may have ever encountered before. This discussion may make some of you uncomfortable. Throughout this book, we'll explore the various religions and teachings that have been passed down through many generations. For many, religion is quite a sacred concept, and understandably, they prefer not to explore any alternative ideas to their concepts. However, since you have chosen this book, and the title literally makes it clear what this book is about, I doubt anyone unprepared for this discussion is still here reading it.

Some of you might close this book, feeling more confused than before, but for others, it will answer many questions. Most of all, I hope that each of you learns something from it and realize the true meaning of the Bible. After all, the Bible is meant to be understood, not merely read.

Let's get something straight before we go any further. I am neither a religious scholar who has studied the Bible for multiple decades, nor have I received any religious training or mentorship. This book reflects what I have been shown over the years. And no, I didn't hear any voices or experience visions that compelled me to take on this endeavor. You see, there have been a number of events in my life where the outcomes could very well have resulted in my death.

Here are a few examples of those events. Once, in my early teens, a friend and I were hunting rabbits. We had crossed one field and were about to cross a fence into the next when my friend stopped dead in his tracks and pointed his .22-caliber rifle at a rabbit, which was roughly twelve feet away. I stopped and watched as he aimed and fired. I heard the crack of the shot and, at the same time, felt something strike my forehead.

"Hey!" I exclaimed, startled and confused.

The rabbit took off, uninjured, because my friend had missed. I knew my friend was an excellent marksman, but at the same time, I was rubbing my forehead in confusion, trying to figure out what had just hit it. As luck would have it for the rabbit, there was a strand of barbed wire between it and my friend's rifle. The bullet struck the strand of barbed wire and ricocheted back at me.

I asked my friend if I was bleeding. "No," he replied. However, he told me that a sizable welt had already formed in the middle of my forehead. I never gave much thought to the idea of guardian angels at that time in my life, but surely, something or someone had intervened in what could have been a deadly accident.

The next event, and possibly the most significant, was when I was a helicopter gunship pilot serving in Vietnam. Our mission was to find the enemy, make contact, and eliminate the enemy operating around the city of Saigon. One of the most dangerous missions we flew was called The Nighthawk Mission. We would send out three helicopters, two of which were gunships and one called Lightship. We flew four two-hour missions in one of the four Saigon sectors.

Flying the Lightship was the most dangerous part of the mission I had ever flown up until that point. You see, consecutively flying the Lightship at night at a very low altitude and airspeed was not the norm for me. We called it flying in the death zone. Throughout my training as a helicopter pilot, I was told that the best way to survive was to fly as high and as fast as possible. However, this mission required the exact opposite, it was a completely different style of flying. In addition, nights in Vietnam were pitch-black, especially in the remote areas we were operating in where there were very few lights on the ground, if any.

Hopefully, you can imagine that flying a helicopter with a very large light mounted on its side, at a very low altitude and airspeed, made us an easy target for the enemy to reveal themselves and a death trap for those inside the Lightship. We were to fly the Lightship every night without fail. Unless we had a maintenance or weather problem, we would take turns flying the Lightship or flying one of the two gunships that would cover the Lightship and return fire should the Lightship receive fire, which was literally the purpose of the Lightship. Yes, we flew in the death zone, knowing the enemy would shoot at us and give away their position. I have no idea how many times I was fired upon. At first, I kept count, but eventually, I stopped.

Any form of combat teaches you things about yourself that no person or book ever could. I had, and still have, a great deal of respect for those I once called my enemy. Much was learned over my time as a pilot. Call it luck or being blessed, we did survive those missions. For me, it was an answer to many, many prayers. Yes, there were a lot of prayers, most of them asking God to keep all of us alive and uninjured and to keep this "bird" in the air. It was an extremely dangerous mission, but I endured, though things could swing in the adverse direction in literally seconds.

My next near-death experience came as a complete surprise. In truth, they all did to a certain extent, but this one was different. It came at a time when I never thought something bad could happen to me. At that time, I was a part-time member of the Army National Guard. It was during the middle weekend of our two-week annual training, and a group of us had decided to go tubing down a river.

Everyone—except for my wife (at that time), a friend of ours, and me—entered the river and started going downstream. The three of us were talking and enjoying our free time. Soon, we saw that the larger group drifting further down with the current, and it was clear that we needed to catch up with them before losing sight of them. The next thing I knew, my ex-wife had already gotten on her tube and was also nearly out of sight, leaving just our friend and myself on the shore.

Not long after we were in our tubes and floating downstream, our friend decided to shove me off my tube for some unknown, peculiar reason and dunk me in the water, forcefully holding me under the water. I thought it was rather odd for him to do this. I struggled and finally got free from his grip within a couple of seconds, resurfaced, and swam back to my tube. When I got to my tube, I saw that my ex-wife was still quite ways ahead of us. It didn't make a lot of sense to be horsing around when we were trying to catch up with the others.

Then, once again, and to my surprise, our friend tipped me over and pulled me down under the water. This was no longer a game because, this time, he was holding me down for as long as he could. I could feel the pressure of his hands forcing me down. Luckily for me, I could hold my breath longer than he could, so when he needed to resurface, I grabbed his leg and, in one quick motion, turned the tables.

I held him down to my level so that when we both resurfaced, he would not be able to get a breath of air before me. I rapidly began swimming to my tube, kicking hard with my feet and using a frantic breaststroke to stay away from him and only finding the courage to stop when he stopped to rest himself. I was very confused, shaken, and disturbed because my ex-wife and I had trusted him, while clearly, something was terribly wrong with him.

To this day, I still don't know why he wanted to end my life. I should have confronted him at the end of the tube trip, but I didn't. He also remained quiet after that incident, confirming that he had some evil intentions. I have my suspicions as to why he did it. Proving his motives would have been somewhat difficult, but I made sure never to let him get me into any kind of situation where he would have the upper hand again.

Like many of you, I've had my share of close calls on the road where there are times in traffic where I encountered reckless drivers who should not be driving at all. Luckily, I've been able to avoid those accidents by near misses and by the grace of God.

It was sometime around 2012 that I realized that I might not have thanked God or my guardian angels enough for watching over me throughout my life. I thought that since God has done so many wonderful things for me, perhaps I should ask God if there was something I could do for him. As the old expression goes, God would never give you more than you can handle. It is my opinion that only God truly understands just how much one can truly handle, and He will guide you through the endevor.

It was about three months after I spoke with God that I awakened at exactly 3:23 in the morning. I had had a question about Jesus earlier that month, one that suddenly started echoing in my mind. There was this strange and strong urge to instantly check for the Bible's answer. Keep in mind that it was after three in the morning, so it made no sense that my mind would suddenly want to find an answer to something. Stranger still, it was the first and only thought that came to mind just before waking. I immediately walked to my desk and got my Bible to satisfy my curiosity. The answer to my question was right before my eyes. It had always been there, but I had not seen it until now.

I can't recall how many days later that I was awakened at around the same hour. All my questions have been answered just like this with an answer that makes far more sense than what I had been taught earlier in my life. The 3:00 a.m. awakenings are well documented as the time frame when the Heavenly Father chooses to reveal something important to people. I do not go back to sleep until I get up and write it down. This occurrence is well known as Brahma Muhurta.

As I mentioned earlier, there are no voices in my head filling my consciousness with random information. It's the truth that I now see. I can now visualize what I couldn't see previously. The Bible has truly become a joy to study. It is full of information about our origin, how we should live our lives now, and how things will end up in the future. Everything is a bit different than I had thought it was supposed to be. Everything seemed new. This fresh perspective makes the Bible far more engaging and pulsing with life.

I hope and pray that I will be able to show you things in the Bible that the Lord has shown me, that many of you have never seen nor been told about. You could say that through my simple literary skills, I'll direct your thoughts toward passages of the Bible that I know people have misinterpreted, are still confused about, and often just give up on figuring it out.

To paraphrase another old expression, I know for a fact that I can please some of the people all the time and please all the people some of the time. If I can at least please some of the people some of the time, this book will have been well worth the effort and stress poured into it. That is what I aim to do, to give a pair of special spectacles to some people for a short duration so they can see what I see. You'll need to have an open mind for this book. Take it or leave it.

Chapter 1
The Bible on Other Gods

What comes to mind when you think about God? If you are religious, you may think of the God you follow and believe in. If you are not religious but come from a religious background, you might think of the God you once believed in. If you simply do not believe in God, you will likely think of the reasoning you use to justify your perspective. These simple distinctions make something quite clear: There is no universal definition of God that captures the individual details. People think of God in many different ways, but that is not, and can never be reflected in a single definition. The reason is the immense variance the term holds on an individual, cultural, and social level.

Now that we have established that the definition of God is multifaceted, we can move on to a more complex dimension. Many people who believe in one or more gods have strict or firmly set rules associated with them. While studying the Bible, I realized that many who claim to follow it have not researched it thoroughly. Whenever I approached a scholar, priest, or anyone presumed well-versed in the Bible, I received different answers to the same question.

Writing a book with serious religious and spiritual themes was not my original intention. Although I grew up in a Christian household, church was not a place I visited often.

During Bible studies, I noticed that the teachers did not actually study the Bible as one would study a book in an English literature class. They did not examine each chapter for its underlying meanings. They did not try to dissect the themes and concepts down to every last detail. With all that said, please remember that the subjects in this book are those that I believe God wants you to know about at this time.

It seems to me that many people do not study all the Bible. They recite their favorite verses or repeat the same principles they have decided are its core teachings. They select the verses they find simplest and easiest to interpret then preach them to the masses. But the Bible needs to be understood, interpreted, and applied. Recitation alone won't take you far. What felt more like a Bible-reading group than a study session eventually led me to think differently—to view its concepts through a new lens. As a military veteran, I returned to my training and applied what I had learned.

I decided to study the Bible as a manual rather than a storybook. Now there's the issue with how the Bible was put together. The Bible is not like a regular book. It's a gathering of many books not exactly in chronological order, especially not the Old Testament As a manual, it became something I turned to whenever something felt off or I felt lost. Reading it as a novel, by contrast, encourages you to get through it quickly so you can prepare for a test. You read because you're required to, with little choice in the matter.

The problem with that approach is that you're unlikely to retain anything substantial, especially if the assignment brings little enjoyment. Studying the Bible is a task, not a casual pastime. People treat it as a book you're supposed to read without asking questions. I realized that if I wanted answers to probing, difficult questions—from "why" rather than merely "how"—I would have to find them myself, supported by prayer.

If you ask a scholar about the Bible's background or history, you might not get a straight answer. The Bible is more straightforward than many assume. If you read it without preconceived notions or beliefs, you'll find that it requires careful, detailed observation. Many church leaders look only at the accepted meanings of the words, but the Bible contains far more than that.

A simple example is the verse "Thou shalt not kill" (Exodus 21:13, KJV), commonly quoted by people who believe in the Bible. It is often used to condemn any act that results in a person's death except by legal authority. But when I first heard it, it didn't sit right with me. I had spent part of my life killing while in Vietnam, but under legal authority. Before you start thinking I'm a psychopath, let me tell you more about myself. I served thirty-two years in the United States Army as a helicopter pilot. My service began when I was drafted during the Vietnam War. Many died on both sides, killed by people who had never killed before. I never considered that a flaw in my character or a stain on my reputation. I served my country and obeyed orders. Killing was not my preferred aspect of service, but I was proud to serve. It was not a way of life—it was a way of staying alive. When it's you on the other end of the barrel, you don't have much choice. Simply put, it's either them or you.

Years later, while discussing my time in Vietnam, someone asked whether I ever felt bad about killing people. Instead of giving the expected answer, I said, "Hell no. It was either them or me." That had always been my attitude. Then someone brought up the verse "Thou shalt not kill," which made me think. At the time, I didn't know much about the Bible, so I didn't have a better answer.

That conversation pushed me to dig deeper. I wanted to know what the Bible actually said. I soon found myself getting down to brass tacks. Was what I did sinful? Was I a sinner even though I had served my country? When I brought my questions to scholars, many had no answer. They deflected or changed the subject. No one could tell me what the Bible really meant, let alone elaborate. That was when I realized the only one who could help me understand the Bible was God. I stopped merely reading it and began studying it. I set aside my preconceived beliefs and focused on what the text actually said. Over time, verses I had never noticed seemed to jump off the page. I read and reread passages. I studied parts of the Bible as if it were a helicopter manual I needed to master. I studied it to answer the questions that kept arising. And what I found was shocking—very different from what I had been told. As I said earlier, the Bible is complex. Its stories and chapters are connected in ways many people never recognize.

Through prayer, research, and study, I learned far more than I expected—more than many people know, even those well-versed in Scripture. Those who claim they have learned everything in the Bible often do not know its full background or how its stories connect. Many believers say there is only one God, the creator of everything in the universe. But through my study that the Lord gave me, I learned that the Bible speaks of more than one God. It never uses the word *universe*—only *Earth* and *heavens*. I had to think about that for a minute, but it's true.

The Bible mentions many gods, each with a name. Some names are even forbidden to speak. One example is the God of the Israelites, whose name is "Yahweh ELOHIYM." His name is said to resemble the sound of the wind howling—a sound humans cannot replicate. For that reason, His name is not to be pronounced; attempting to do so may even be considered disrespectful. Ok, question? How do you pray to a God whose name you are not supposed to use? Sounds tricky, or maybe it was added by man. I had to think about that also. Well, lucky for us Christians, we can speak the name of our God. The God of the Christians is YAHUSHA. You know him better as Jesus. More about that later in the book.

There are many different Gods in the Bible. Where did that come from, you ask? It's found in Deuteronomy 13:1–11:

> Suppose a prophet or one who foretells by dreams appeared among you and showed you a sign or wonder, and the sign or wonder should come to pass concerning what he said to you, namely 'Let us follow other Gods. Gods who you have not previously known and let us serve them.' You must not listen to the words of that prophet or dreamer, for the Lord your God will be testing you to see if you love Him with all your mind and being. (NET Bible, Reader's Edition)

As you read this, you will encounter mentions of other gods. There is one passage in particular that proves—beyond a shadow of a doubt—that there is more than one God.

Our God wrote on stone tablets and gave them to Moses to share with the Israelites. These tablets contained the Ten Commandments. In the very first commandment, God writes, "Have no other gods before me." If our own God acknowledges the existence of other gods, who am I to insist otherwise—much less expect you to believe there is only one god?

One thing everyone should understand is that the Bible has been edited over the centuries. The original text has changed through translation and through the influence of various authorities. Although its core remains intact, its wording and context have shifted. This is why what we read in the Bible today may not be exactly what our ancestors read centuries ago.

It is also important to know that the Old Testament is composed of selected books from the Jewish Torah. It comes from the Torah but is not the complete Torah. Each book included in the Old Testament had to go through a vetting process known as the canonization process, which took place at the Council of Laodicea in AD 363–366. Using this process, those in charge undertook the considerable task of narrowing down the Torah into a more user–friendly version of what we now call the Old Testament.

As with any major project, someone eventually proposes a different idea. Today we have an Eastern Holy Bible and a Western Holy Bible. The Ethiopian Bible—the Eastern Bible—is the oldest and most original. The two versions are similar in most respects, except that the Western Bible removed five books from the Old Testament. The Eastern Bible still uses the name *ELOHIYM*, while the Western Bible replaced *ELOHIYM* with "*God*."

In one of the older versions I studied, a verse read, "In the beginning, *ELOHIYM* created the heavens and earth." If you have read newer translations, you may understandably be confused, because they read, "In the beginning, God created the heavens and the earth." What did this discovery teach me? I learned that *ELOHIYM* is a plural term referring to gods. Further research showed that more than one God could have been involved in creating the heavens and the Earth. I had to stop and think about this, and as I studied, I found more answers to justify my thinking.

This may come as a surprise. Our God's name is not *God*. *God* is not a name; it is a title. Our God's name is *Yahweh ELOHIYM* (Genesis 2:4, Cepher). Consider the first chapter of Genesis in the older text. It uses *ELOHIYM* to describe those who carried out the six days of Creation— opening the possibility that more than one god was involved. Then, in

Genesis 2:4, we are introduced to *Yahweh Elohiym*. Throughout the Bible, various verses use the word God in reference to ELOHIYM—or to several gods. This led me to believe that there is more than one God.

This is interesting. The only Bible that I found that says that YAHWEH ELOHIYM also created people on the Sixth Day of Creation, and that is the last time they are mentioned. Wonder what happen to them.

Have you been counting? So far,there have been at least two things that some, if not most of you, have never known are in the Bible and for some, maybe more.

Then there is Malachi 2:10–12 (The Jerusalem Bible), which discusses a very interesting factor. The verse said,

> Have we not all one Father? Did not one God create us? Why, then, do we break faith with one another, profaning the covenant of our ancestors? Judah has broken faith; a detestable thing has been done (in Israel and) in Jerusalem. Yes, Judah has profaned the sanctuary that Yahweh loves. He has married the daughter of an alien god. Israelites were not to marry others that were not Israelites.

Not many people seem to grasp it because of how it has changed throughout the new versions of the Bible. Thus, even in Malachi, God tells us that there were alien gods in this verse.

It is important to note that chapter 2 of Genesis introduces us to our God, Yahweh Elohiym (Cepher). He is the God who created Adam and Eve and became known as the God of the Israelites. This occurred after the

Seven Days of Creation. The Israelites were not created on the sixth day like the others were by their own gods.

Keep this in mind when you later read that Cain had to leave his home and travel to the land of Nod, where he feared the "others" might harm him because of what he had done to his brother. Who created these "other" people—such as Cain's wife? Remember also that he took a wife who belonged to a different God in the land of Nod. (See chapter 5 for more detail.)

If you were to read the entire chapter, you would see references to an "alien" or "foreign" God. Judah profaned the sanctuary Yahweh loves by marrying a woman who believed in and worshipped an alien God—meaning he married outside the Israelites.

We also see in Acts 14:8–12 (KJV) that Paul was preaching the Gospel in Lystra when a crippled man was healed after Paul told him, "Stand upright on thy feet." The man immediately leapt up and walked. Witnesses declared it a miracle and insisted that Paul and Barnabas be renamed Hermes and Zeus. Even in that small village, the people considered Hermes and Zeus to be Gods.

So, does that mean the Bible acknowledges the possibility—perhaps even the truth—of other gods? If the examples above are not enough, reconsider the very first commandment of the Ten Commandants, given by the God of the Israelites. Everything in the Bible is connected in one way or another. If you were to keep an open mind and allow yourself to question what you read and that does not sound quite right, you would find that the truth is right there in plain sight.

Part of my purpose in writing this book is to shed light on the past and present writings in the Bibles. I wanted to compare what I once believed with what I know, have been shown, and believe now. These are my studies, my discoveries after receiving the information from the Lord. They remain open to your own discretion. I am sharing the thoughts and conclusions I reached through my research. What led me in the direction of writing this book? There are several reasons.

I wrote this book because there are things about the Bible that not everyone talks about. It is not an easy topic to read or discuss. People often become uncomfortable or even offended. My intention is neither to unsettle, nor to provoke anyone. I want to help you see the Bible the way that the Lord has presented it to me, and to present it to you.—to look at it with focus and open-mindedness.

On its surface, the Bible may seem contradicting or confusing. Also understand that there appears to be a lack of standardization. But if you put time and effort into it—asking the "How?" "Why?" and "Who?" questions—you begin to understand it differently. Everyone seeks salvation. Religion can be a tricky part of one's spiritual life because one must tread carefully, or risk never reaching that salvation. Religion is not the same as spirituality. Religions are organized groups in which those in authority may use a holy book—and the God they follow—to steer their agendas. They use certain verses to support their perspectives. Many people choose to believe what they are told and follow it blindly.

Who would dare argue with a religious scholar who seems to know more than we do? That is why God wants you to read the Bible and not be guided by preconceived notions or information. Read the older printed Bibles, with an open mind and a clear head. Do not rely solely on others' ideas about religion or who God is. Take notes. Collect your own findings. Study it like a manual, and the underlying messages God wants you to know will reveal themselves. Check everything for yourself and keep the good.

That is the way to reach the true core of the Bible—through study, time, and effort. If you study it like a manual and examine every chapter and verse, you will form a deeper connection with it. Then, when you make decisions, they will be rooted in your own insights, supported by your own research within the text. You will know who God is to you and what He does for you. You will understand what He has done, what He continues to do, and the path He wants you to walk upon. You will also learn what He asks of you. You will learn more about yourself and the world than any other medium could teach. I truly believe you will learn what I am showing to you and what God wants you to learn; therefore, brace yourself for the power of truth.

Earlier, I mentioned other gods because this is what I've been shown. What we now know is that, in the beginning, the planet was a sphere— not flat, as earlier people believed. The regions of the world were divided among different Gods, who placed their people in lands of their choosing, according to their own image and likeness of that God. For example, one or more gods chose Northern Africa, for example like the areas of Canaan Egypt, Babylonia Arabia; one or more gods chose Europe for the Norsemen, Vikings; one or more chose Australia for the Aboriginal peoples; and one or more chose the Americas for the Native Americans; North, Central and South. There were also the island peoples, and many more. These gods instructed their people to be fruitful and multiply—and they did. These people were not descendants of Adam and Eve. Adam and Eve were created later in the Second Story of Creation, some 786 miles away, if it were a straight line of travel. That is West southwest of what is now called Israel. *See* map.

Do you ever wonder what the Bible wants us to understand when it says "in their likeness" and "in their image"? Could it be that the various gods themselves differ in skin color, eye color, hair, and body structure? Think about it.

For years, I have pondered what is meant by "in their likeness" and "in their image." This is simply what I have been shown, but to me, it means that we resemble the God who created us more than we resemble the other gods. You may want to pause here and take time to absorb this because this is what the gods want you to understand. See, it's good to question and think about it.

Chapter 2
The Greatest Puzzle of All Time

When my hand brushed the cardboard, previously invisible dust lifted into the air. The early morning sunlight pouring through the single basement window illuminated the drifting specks, each catching a brief second in the spotlight. I set the rectangular box on the table and sat down across from it. I only had a vague idea of what I was undertaking, yet I continued with every intention of winning. With determination at its peak, I lifted the cardboard lid.

As the cover separated from the bottom, a short burst of air sent the resting dust airborne again. I slid the lid under the table and stared at my enemy—my personal Mount Everest. I stared at the tiny pieces of cardboard I had never attempted to connect before. *That changes today*, I told myself. "Today, I will overcome one of my childhood challenges."

Puzzles are not a bed of roses. Solving them requires hard work, determination, and concentration. Many people approach them with high morale, ready to conquer the innocent-looking pieces, only to fold in the process. Yet, puzzles remain fun for many around the world. Some people complete several every week. Together, we will see whether we can piece together "the greatest puzzle of all time" by studying the Bible.

What does the Bible tell us about the beginning, about living our lives, and about how it all ends—if it ends at all? Over the years, I have discussed specific passages with many pastors. When questions arise about the meaning of a word or verse, the answer often hinges on how that word was translated. More importantly, a single word can carry multiple meanings, and context adds another layer of complexity.

For example, someone may gift you a puzzle—or in this case, a Bible—but the peculiar thing about the Bible puzzle is that it comes with no reference photo. When you begin, you quickly realize how much more challenging the task becomes without a visual guide. This brings me back to my point: When the early humans first interpreted the words of God, they placed pieces of the puzzle wherever they thought they might fit, using only the knowledge available to them. Over time, they shifted pieces around and produced a nearly complete picture, though several pieces were left unused. Our predecessors likely completed the edges first and filled in the interior with whatever seemed to make sense. As a result, the leftover fragments—the missing information and forgotten knowledge—never saw the light of day or became part of the puzzle. Whatever picture was completed then became the truth, so long as it did not conflict with the beliefs of the powerful.

This is where my theory comes in. The picture we were told was complete still has missing information. Those missing pieces remain in the box—the Bible, in this analogy. As time passed, people began to sense that something was absent. They realized the picture was only partially completed and started adding in forgotten pieces. Many people reject newer versions of the Bible and cling to older editions, assuming they are less likely to have been altered. As you continue reading this book, I will point out the many ways human hands have tampered with Scripture.

People may believe whatever they choose, but in my view, all the puzzle pieces have always been there. We simply did not know what the puzzle was supposed to look like, especially without a visual guide. The Bible also contains many hidden and subtle references that are not meant to be taken literally. For example, the commandment "Thou shalt not kill" (Exodus 20:13, KJV) may not mean what some people assume. If a psychopath entered my home and threatened my family, I would not stand aside—I would defend them, as any endangered person would.

Now that this is established, it is important to note that additions and omissions throughout history have created confusion. With so many versions available, people often do not know which Bible is the most reliable. On top of that, Scripture is filled with layered meanings, references, and analogies that require interpretation. You might think that asking a preacher or scholar is the best way to get answers, but interpretation is influenced by life experience, prejudice, gender, class, and ethnicity. Naturally, interpretations vary widely.

The last Bible widely regarded as the standard was the King James Version, first printed in 1611. It became the principal Bible of nearly all Christian churches and is still used in many congregations today. It is likely the version you will find in the pews before you.

But what is the value of a standard Bible? You cannot complete a puzzle if your pieces come from different boxes. Standardization—whether in Scripture or anything else we rely on—is essential to our clarity and peace of mind. Imagine spending hours on a puzzle only to discover that extra pieces from another set were mixed in. That is essentially what has happened to the Christian Bible over the last seventy years. We went from one widely accepted version to more than 120 new ones.

So, what happened to the warning in Revelation 22:18–19 (KJV)?

For I testify unto every man that heareth the words of the prophecy of this book, If any man shall add unto these things, God shall add unto him the plagues that are written in this book: And if any man shall take away from the words of the book of this prophecy, God shall take away his part out of the book of life…

This is yet another reason God wants you to read Scripture for yourself. If you believe a religious leader is not truly following the Bible, you have every right to ask them where, exactly, they found their claims. This is the beauty of Church. When two or more are gathered in His name to discuss church community issues defines the meaning of church.

In the end, some pieces have been forcefully pressed into the puzzle simply because they appear to fit or someone wanted them to fit them there. Those not-quite-right pieces are the ones I pursue. Many say that millions of believers cannot have been wrong for so many years—but can they? I maintain that when the correct piece of a puzzle fits, it falls into place naturally. The lines between the pieces disappear.

Chapter 3
In the Beginning

Have you ever created something? It may seem like a foolish question—of course, you have. As children, many of us made airplanes out of paper, Frisbees out of paper plates, or slime from white glue. All these simple crafts share one thing: each is made from something. Everything around us is formed from simpler components or raw materials.

This brings me back to my earlier question: If we can create, does that make us gods? Many religions define God as the force capable of creating. Yet humans also create. Doesn't that mean we possess an attribute associated with divinity? Let me clarify why this idea matters. Yes, humans are gifted with intelligence and the ability to create, but our creative power is vastly different from that of the gods. We can create *something out of something*. They create *something out of nothing*. This concept is known as *creatio ex nihilo.*

Ex nihilo is Latin for "out of nothing." This idea appears in most theistic religions—belief systems in which God or the gods are supreme over all matter. The premise is that one eternal being, or a group of them, has always existed and always will. These beings brought into existence everything we know, whether physical or intangible. Evidence of Creation exists far beyond what the human eye can perceive. Keep that in mind.

The essential point is this: Only the god(s) have demonstrated the power to create something out of nothing. One major example is the Creation of the world itself. God(s) made the heavens and the Earth and placed within them every living creature, including us. They created everything in the six days of creation with no preexisting substance. It is astonishing when you consider it—something wholly nonexistent, with no blueprint, brought into being from nothing. It defies human comprehension.

Humans cannot create in this way. Even our ideas come from something. Everything we imagine echoes what already exists, whether fully formed or in a primitive version. The Wright brothers, credited with inventing the first successful flying machine, relied upon available components—and their idea was inspired by birds and other flying creatures. Humans cannot imagine something that has no basis in reality, let alone create it from materials that do not exist.

Before moving forward, I want to note that I will not rely on only one Bible. As mentioned earlier, there are more than 120 versions of the Holy Bible. For the purposes of this book, I have chosen just a few to reference.

They are as follows:
1. The Net Bible, Reader's Edition
2. The Holy Bible, King James Version
3. The Guidepost Parallel Bible, which consists of The King James Version, The Modern Language Bible, The Living Bible, and The Revised Standard Version
4. The Jerusalem Bible
5. The Cepher

"Why more than one Bible?" you might ask. Simply put, each version offers a different way of examining the puzzle pieces so you can find the one that fits. This is not fair, we should NOT have to examine so many bibles. This is a big problem and causes people of different religious groups the inability to communicate on the same level with different information.

What I am about to explain is not something I invented, though I sometimes wish it were. Much of it came from early-morning awakenings—Brahma Muhurta—moments when I felt as though I was being handed yet another piece of the puzzle.

I will begin with Genesis 1:1. I am about to show you things many people have never noticed, even though they have been in the Bible the entire time. The best place to begin is, indeed, "In the Beginning." Interestingly, the NET Bible titles this section "The Creation of the World."

What does "In the Beginning" mean to you? Some believe it refers to the beginning of time. Others think of the big bang theory. Some say it encompasses both. But what does the Bible actually tell us? When you read the entire verse, it is clear that it refers specifically to the creation of the heavens and the Earth.

As noted earlier, the Bible never discusses the universe. Instead, it focuses on the formation of our planet—which, according to the text, was round from the beginning, even though early people believed otherwise. The verse also identifies who created the Earth: "ELOHIYM created the Earth and the Heavens" (Genesis 1:1, Cepher). ELOHIYM is another name for "gods." Early manuscripts used this word, but later versions replaced *ELOHIYM* with *God* to promote the belief in a single deity. For a long time, these changes shaped people's understanding. However, the Old Testament draws directly from the Jewish Torah, which still uses the word *ELOHIYM*.

Notice something else: "In the beginning, Elohiym created the heavens." Not only does the text identify more than one God, it also refers to more than one heaven—something I discussed earlier in chapter 1.

Elohim (Hebrew: מיהלֱא, romanized: ʾĔlōhīm: [(?) eloˈ(h)im]), the plural of אלוהֱ (ʾĔlōah), is a Hebrew word meaning "gods" or "godhood". Although the word is plural, in the Hebrew Bible it most often takes singular verbal or pronominal agreement and refers to a single deity. The word elohim or ʿELOHIYM (ʾĕlôhîym) is a grammatically plural noun for "Gods" or "deities" or various other words in Biblical Hebrew.

Genesis, specifically chapter 1:2, is a little bit tricky. This is where religion and science seem to take different paths. Yet science has continued to advance, and the formation of our planet is no longer a matter of debate. As the verse notes, the Earth was "without form and void," and "darkness was upon the face of the deep."

At this early stage of Creation, a great deal of debris surrounded the planet, blocking light from the Sun. Then God caused this debris to fall to Earth—much of it ice crystals. When God said, "Let there be light," light appeared as sunlight broke through to the planet's surface. The next verses describe how God created light for the day; the far side of the planet remained dark, and God called the darkness night. If we asked scientists what was happening during this time, they might say the planet was beginning to take shape.

The fact that God created day and night often leads readers to assume the Bible is referring to an Earth Day. This needs clarification. An Earth

Day is twenty-four Earth hours. A "God Day," however, is said to last a thousand Earth years (2 Peter 3:8, KJV). A day of Creation may have lasted several hundred thousand—or even millions of Earth years. "Evening came, and morning came—the first day of Creation."

At first, I thought I was rambling when drawing a distinction between a twenty-four-hour Earth Day and a day of Creation, but the more I read the Bible, the more confident I became. The first day of Creation ended with evening and morning; it did not begin with morning. It began with God settling the debris and allowing sunlight to reach Earth's surface.

What is time, and do we truly need it? Time has a purpose: to prevent everything that will happen from happening at once. Before timekeeping existed, how did early people manage? When we talk about time, we usually mean Earth's days, weeks, months, and years. But the Bible requires clearer distinctions among Earth time, God's time, and Creation time. Many believe a day of Creation unfolded within an Earth Day, yet we should be honest and let science help us understand how long the Earth's formation would have taken.

"The evening and the morning were the first day." I always felt it should have been written as "the evening and the morning were the first day of creation." Then again, there I go, trying to make things simpler.

I'm also going to share something I recently learned—something many people have never seen or heard before. And as always, please don't shoot the messenger.

In the beginning, over time, there would become

- seven gods of creation,
- seven heavens,
- seven continents,
- seven seas,

- seven races,

- seven religions, and

- seven deadly sins.

You will not find most of these details explicitly in the Bible. All you really need is a map or globe of Earth. Just what does this have to do with the story of creation? As we go through the story of creation at the end of the seventh day, I realize that all seven items I previously listed are somehow intertwined with the seven days of creation. Keep these in mind and see if you can recognize the connection.

The Second Day of Creation involves the separation of waters. The water above—likely mist or clouds—rose from the waters below, forming the sky. This day also marks the formation of Earth's atmosphere, giving us the air we breathe. Evening and morning concluded the second day. Another Bible (Genesis 14:17, The Cepher) refers to the space between lower and upper waters as where the heaven or heavens are located. Could the sky, or better yet our atmosphere itself, be Heaven?

The Third Day of Creation was busy. Water receded, allowing land to appear, producing vegetation and plants yielding seeds. This likely involved great geological activity—earthquakes and volcanoes. The gathered waters were called seas, and God saw that it was good.

On the Fourth Day of Creation, the gods established what we now measure as Earth time. The sun rules the day; the moon rules the night. The Earth was set spinning and tilted on its axis, determining days, seasons, and years. This tilt allowed vegetation to flourish beyond the equator. Evening and morning concluded the fourth day, and God saw that it was good.

The Fifth Day of Creation brought living creatures. Waters filled with swarms of life, birds flew above the Earth, and all creatures were created according to their kinds—including birds that cannot fly. Each was commanded to be fruitful, multiply, and fill the waters and sky. Evening and morning marked the fifth day, and God saw that it was good.

The Sixth Day of Creation was extraordinary. Dinosaurs emerged, though the Bible does not mention them by name. Land animals—cattle, wild animals, and creeping things—were created. Fossil evidence even suggests that human remains coexisted with some dinosaur fossils. Genesis 1:26 states, "Let us make man in our image, after our likeness: and let them have dominion over the fish of the sea, and over the fowl of the air, and over the cattle, and over all the earth, and over every creeping thing that creepeth upon the earth" (KJV).

Notice the plural, "let us make man"—indicating multiple gods were involved in Creation. God(s) blessed humankind, instructing them to be fruitful, multiply, and rule over living things. This also explains the seven races and seven continents. People were placed simultaneously across North America, South America, Europe, Asia, Australia, Africa, and the Island nations.

Humans were given dominion over creatures that breathe air and the fish that live in water. So next time someone cites "Thou shalt not kill" to prevent hunting or fishing, remember that this commandment refers to humans, not animals.

Recapping the sixth day, it suggests the existence of more than one God, shows God(s) blessing humanity to be fruitful and multiply, and granting dominion over living things. No Tree of Life or Tree of Knowledge is mentioned, nor are any names given. Six days passed—how many Earth years is unknown, but likely thousands or millions. God saw all that He had made, and it was very good.

Chapter 2 of Genesis tells us that Creation was complete. All work ceased on the seventh day. God(s) blessed the seventh day and made it holy. Remember, the seventh day was still a day of Creation, not an Earth day. I will discuss the Sabbath in greater detail later.

Supporting Verses for the First Story of Creation

The first account, found in Genesis chapter 1, walks us through Elohiym's seven days of the Creation journey as they created everything (The Cepher Bible).

"And God said, let there be light: and there was light." This was day 1 (Genesis 1:3, The Holy Bible, KJV).

Following the above verse, other verses explain how God separated the light from the darkness.

"And God called the firmament Heaven. And the evening and the morning were the second day." This is day 2 (chapter 1:8 *Id.*).

Then, the land was separated from the water: "And God said, Let the earth bring forth grass, the herb yielding seed, and the fruit tree yielding fruit after his kind, whose seed is in itself, upon the earth; and it was so." This was day 3 (chapter 1:11 *Id.*).

Next, God gave time and direction to the world through seasons, days, and years.

"And God made two great lights; the greater light to rule the day and the lesser light to rule the night: he made the stars also." This was day 4 (chapter 1:16 *Id.*).

God then allowed light to rule the day and darkness to rule the night.

"And God said, Let the waters bring forth abundantly the moving creatures that hath life, and fowl that may fly above the earth in the open firmament of heaven." This was day 5 (Genesis1:20 *Id*).

God then commanded the creatures to reproduce and spread their kind all over the planet.

"And God said, let the earth bring forth the living creatures after his kind, cattle, and creeping thing, and beast of the earth after his kind: and it was so." This was day 6 (Genesis 1:26 *Id.*).

Then God ordered them to copulate. Remember, humans were then given dominion over all other creatures present.

"And God saw everything that he had made, and behold, it was very good. And the evening and the morning were the Sixth Day." This was also day 6 (Genesis 1:31 *Id.*).

On the last of the days of Creation, the Seventh Day of Creation, God saved for rest and to look back at the magnificent creation that had been created out of nothing.

Chapter 4
The Second Story of Creation

Let's now delve deeper into the two stories of Creation to better understand *creatio ex nihilo* and its first practical application. As you may know, the Bible contains two creation stories. As a Christian, I believe this is how the world came to be, though I recognize that other religions may have different accounts. I am not claiming this is the only truth—only that this is what I have been given to share.

Not all Bibles label it as the "second story of creation." Some refer to it as the creation of man and woman. But wait—didn't we already discuss the creation of man and woman on the Sixth Day of Creation? Yes, we did, or so I thought. Remember when I mentioned the seven races and seven continents?

On the sixth day, people were placed across the planet in their new homes, given necessities to flourish and grow. Many Earth years passed. Populations increased, some began governing themselves with laws and traditions, and a few developed their own religions. The second story of Creation is not about these already existing people.

This second story introduces us to a God of the Elohiym. This God has a name: Yahuah Elohiym. Throughout this book, I will refer to Him simply as God. From this point, the Bible focuses primarily on one God and the man and woman He created. The people from the first story lived near rivers, lakes, and seas because those were their food sources. Rain had not yet fallen on the land, plants and trees could not grow, and no one had been taught to till the soil.

Before Adam was created, NO one had the knowledge of how to till the soil and take care of plants and animals. Adam was given the purpose to cultivate the land and grow food. God formed man from the soil, breathed the breath of life into his nostrils, and the man became a living being. God then brought this man to a special garden in the eastern part of Eden—a garden made especially for him. At this point, no woman exists yet. How many of you knew that Adam had a purpose?

God named the man "Adam." Adam learned to care for the garden's plants, trees and animals. God noticed that it was not good for Adam to be alone, so He created animals and birds for companionship. Adam was tasked with naming all the plants, animals and birds. Yet despite all these companions, something was missing: a mate.

Notice the difference: In the first story, male and female were created together on the sixth day, but in this story, a period of time separates the creation of Adam and the creation of Eve. Here, Eve is made from one of Adam's ribs—a detail not mentioned in the first story. Its importance seems significant since it is highlighted here.

Supporting Verses for the Second Story of Creation

The second account is considered more of a complimentary description than an alternative. In Genesis chapter 2, this story contradicts the first one, confusing many to this day.

"And the Lord God formed man of the dust of the ground and breathed into his nostrils the breath of life, and man became a living soul" (Genesis 2:7, KJV).

God made Adam and determined a place for his dwelling, The Garden of Eden: "And out of the ground made the Lord God to grow every tree that is pleasant to the sight, and good for food; the tree of life also in the midst of the garden, and the tree of knowledge of good and evil" (Genesis 2:9 *Id*).

After man was created, God erected plants and trees on Earth, with a river to sustain the natural ecosystem there.

"And out of the ground the Lord God formed every beast of the field and every fowl of the air; and brought them unto Adam to see what he would call them: and whatsoever Adam called every living creature that was the name thereof" (Genesis 2:19 *Id*).

After man was settled, the Lord had creatures materialized from the ground. After this, Adam was placed into a deep slumber.

"And the rib, which the Lord God had taken from man, made he a woman and brought her unto the man" (Genesis 2:22 *Id*).

This is where man and woman were first united.

"And on the seventh day God ended his work which he had made, and he rested on the seventh day from all his work which he had made" – (Genesis 2:2 *Id*).

"And God blessed the seventh day and sanctified it: because that in it he had rested from all his work which God created and made" (Genesis 2:3 *Id*).

Everything was made, and God stepped back to see all the work He had done. Verses 2:2 and 2:3 appear to be placed at the start of the passage, although they describe the end. There could be hidden wisdom behind this. This was the chronology of events for the creation story outlined in Genesis, chapter 2.

The Differences Between the Two Stories of Creation

Even if you've never heard of these two creation accounts, I am confident you've noticed discrepancies. If you haven't, perhaps you have not been paying as close attention as you should. Among the many differences, the most significant is chronological order. In Genesis 1, it appears that plants were made first, followed by animals, and lastly, humans. In the second narrative, however, man was placed in the Garden of Eden, then plants were made to sprout from the terrain, followed by animals. There is another sequential difference regarding men and women. In Genesis 1, male and female were created simultaneously, while in Genesis 2, Adam was alone for a time before he was put to sleep, and a rib was taken from him to create the woman we now call Eve. Reference verses for all these can be found above.

There are, of course, more contradictions that I have not addressed here. As I mentioned in the previous chapter, those in power have adjusted the Bible over time to reflect a view that aligns with their own or that does not contradict their discourse. This means that you can never be certain which parts of the Bible you were taught as a child may have been altered. Perhaps I will never find an explanation for the contradictions or for the newer information absent from older versions of the Bible. This has neither demotivated me nor should it demotivate you from reading and spending your time in pursuit of knowledge.

Returning to the thoughts I discussed in chapter 2, it is important to understand, ponder, and reflect on the subtle verses of holy scripture, but always remember that interpretation varies from person to person. Scrutinize and evaluate. Do not simply assume. This is the only way to find those missing pieces—the forgotten puzzle pieces of supreme literature. Many of us will find this statement incomplete, as prayer remains the most important part of obtaining answers.

Lilith and Adam

According to many sources, including the Jewish Torah, Lilith was Adam's first wife. However, there are contradictions regarding why there are two different origin events for the first woman.

Lilith is considered a haughty goddess, leaving a trail of chaos and destruction through her skill in the art of seduction. She was united with Adam as his wife, but she tried to sow seeds of impurity in him, and so she was replaced by Eve. This, of course, implies that Lilith resented both Adam and Eve. She is portrayed as a half-serpent, half-human being. Some argue that she is the serpent mentioned in Genesis 3, though others disagree. Lilith is a goddess and, according to some traditions, was the wife of Yahweh.

"The serpent was more subtle than any of the wild beasts that Yahweh God had made. It asked the woman, 'Did God really say you were not to eat from any of the trees in the garden?'" (Genesis 3:1, The Jerusalem Bible).

Here, the serpent—or Lilith—attempts to deceive her foe, Eve. The serpent lies about the tree from which God had forbidden them to eat, claiming that it would grant Adam and Eve immortality. Eve convinced Adam, and they both ate the sweet-tasting fruit. Instantly, they realized they were naked and attempted to cover their bodies with whatever foliage they could find. God then asked Adam why he had eaten from the forbidden tree, to which Adam replied, "And the man said, the woman whom thou gavest to be with me, she gave me of the tree, and I did eat" (Genesis 3:12, KJV).

God then addressed the woman:

"And the Lord God said unto the woman, 'What is this that thou hast done?' And the woman said, 'The serpent beguiled me, and I did eat'" (Genesis 3:13, KJV).

God then cursed the serpent, Lilith. Lilith is named and portrayed differently across various religions. Whatever the interpretation, she is shown as a being who continues to exist and walk the Earth, spreading chaos and sowing seeds of immorality and transgression in her former lover's descendants. It took me some time to fully understand what is happening in this story.

The following points have helped me better grasp the narrative:

1. God created Adam to cultivate the soil. Until then, no man had been taught how to do so.

2. The first woman that became known to Adam was a goddess—Lilith (according to the Jewish Torah)—and that relationship did not succeed.

3. The next woman for Adam was created from one of Adam's ribs.

4. There had to be a special reason for Adam and Eve. Had they obeyed God's command and not eaten from either of the two trees in the center of the garden—the Tree of Life and the Tree of the Knowledge of Good and Evil—they would still be alive today, teaching us about good and evil.

5. More than likely, they would also still be living in the garden.

Think about it. To me, this illuminates the differences between the two stories of creation.

Chapter 5
Cain

After Adam and Eve left the Garden, they had two sons, Cain and Abel. I can almost picture these two boys out in the fields, tending the soil and growing food—but wait, Cain is the only one in the field. Where is Abel? Abel is caring for animals, most likely goats and sheep. How could such a simple division of labor lead to so much trouble?

The story of Cain has always fascinated me. I will share it so you can see what I see. It begins as a continuation of the second creation story, which we discussed in the previous chapter.

The Lord God created Adam because the inland area was barren, and nothing would grow there. God wanted someone to cultivate the soil and produce grain and other crops. He provided artisan wells and caused it to rain on the land. Yet before Adam could begin the work he was created for, he got into trouble for eating the prohibited fruit.

"And unto Adam he said, Because thou hast harkened unto the voice of thy wife and hast eaten from the tree, of which I commanded thee, saying, Thou shalt not eat of it, cursed is the ground for thy sake; in sorrow shalt thou eat of it all the days of thy life. Thorns and thistles shall it bring forth to thee; and thou shalt eat the herb of the field. In the sweat of thy face shalt thou eat bread, till thou return unto the ground; for out of it was thou taken; for dust thou art, and to dust shalt thou return" (Genesis 3:17–19, KJV).

This marked the end of paradise. Adam and Eve were sent out of paradise as a consequence of their actions. Cain was the elder son and Abel the younger. The boys grew, learning as much as they could from Adam. They became skilled in their respective callings: Cain in cultivating the soil, Abel in raising livestock.

At a designated time, both boys were to bring offerings to the Lord. Cain brought some of the fruit of the ground, while Abel brought the firstborn of his flock—the healthiest among them. The Lord was pleased with Abel's offering but not with Cain's, because Cain had given only part of his harvest, while Abel gave the best of what he had.

I have thought about it a lot. If the Lord had created Adam primarily to cultivate the soil, and Cain followed in his father's footsteps, why would God favor Abel's offering over Cain's? I know, I am questioning myths and stories that have endured since the days of Adam—but hear me out.

As the story goes, Cain killed Abel. We must try to understand the motive behind this act. The most obvious reason is jealousy.

"And be not like Cain, who belonged to the evil one and murdered his brother. And for what reason did he murder him? Because his own deeds were wicked, and those of his brother were righteous" (1 John 3:12, Modern Language Bible).

Why did God not favor Cain's offering? It is simple if you look closely. God tests His most intelligent creations often. At the time of Adam, there was no exception. These trials are meant to guide humanity toward wisdom, to see who truly believes and remains steadfast under pressure, and who succumbs to evil at the slightest misfortune. Trials distinguish good from evil, the wise from the foolish.

Because his offering was rejected, a seed of evil planted itself in Cain's mind. This seed grew into a destructive force. Instead of reflecting and considering his options, Cain reacted to his jealousy and anger. He murdered Abel. Doubt and evil thoughts are natural; the challenge lies in resisting the urge to act on them. Cain failed.

Cain's actions mirror human behavior even today. When hurt or angered, people often lash out verbally or physically. It is wiser to approach trials calmly. Was it Abel's fault that God favored his offering? Would killing Abel change God's choice? The answer to both is an unequivocal no. Killing Abel did not improve anything; it made things a lot worse. Cain would never be able to live the same life again, and no one would ever see him in the same light again. He was literally the person who showed the world that murder was an actual possibility. Imagine how many murders have been committed from that point to the current time. All those could be on Cain's shoulders.

Jealousy is a dangerous emotion. If nurtured, it can overpower and override your conscience, leading you to behave in ways that damage the person you envy. At the same time, jealousy is a perfectly normal emotion to experience. At some point, you will feel it. The key is to push it out when it inevitably arises. If you do not, it will remain, wreaking havoc on your insides—especially your mental health.

Let us return to Cain and Abel's unfortunate tragedy. Because of the murder he committed, Cain's entire life changed. He was no longer seen as the noble son of Adam. In fact, he was later replaced by another child. Adam and Eve had another son after this incident after Cain left, whom they named Seth. Eve claimed that Seth was the replacement for Cain, who had been sent away by God; therefore, Cain no longer had a place in his family.

Cain was struck with multiple problems and complexities at once because of his actions. He had to leave his home and the land where it was located. Furthermore, he was unable to cultivate the soil as before. It no longer yielded even close to what it had prior to the incident. He was also afraid of the Lord, so he tried to hide from Him—though it did not matter where he hid, for the Lord knew everything. Lastly, what troubled this homeless wanderer most was the fear that others might punish him for his evil deed. He dreaded that he would face the same fate as his brother Abel—death. Above all, he feared others discovering the truth.

Others? Who were these people, and where did they come from? Based on what we learned earlier, you can decide for yourself. I been shown that they were people created during the Sixth Day of Creation. After leaving his land, life, and family behind, Cain began anew in a land called Nod where he married a woman, and together they had daughters. This raises the question: How did this woman come to be there? Cain, who was supposed to live the life of a nomad, was instead building a city. He named the city after his first son, Enoch.

There are a couple of takeaways from this chapter worth mentioning. First, rejection feels bad, but wishing harm to your competitor or the person who rejected you is not the way forward. One should find a smarter, non-aggressive method to rise above. Second, you must learn from your mistakes and beat the competition at their own game by becoming wiser and more experienced. If you truly want to succeed, you must never give up. Get back up after falling. You will fail multiple times in life, but one day it will all pay off. Keep at it, and never wish harm to anyone simply because they perform better than you at something.

Similarly, never let evil decide your destiny. Evil will always be present. It will be like an outstretched arm, pulling you down and sending you plummeting into darkness. Instead, rectify your mistakes to normalize the situation. Cain was probably not angry at Abel; rather, he may have been upset at the outcome of the Lord God's decision. Neither Cain nor Abel were evil people. Cain was simply unable to resist evil. This is how evil works: it makes people do the wrong things. Do not do evil to anyone.

Cain's anger, rage, and jealousy allowed evil to breed in his mind, corrupting him and leading to his downfall. Life is like a bumpy road. There will be ups and downs. During your ups, express gratitude and compassion. During your downs, remain grateful and compassionate, and push away evil thoughts.

Chapter 6
The Tithe

Are you, like me, tired of hearing about this? There is never enough money to meet all the needs of a church. If there is enough, suddenly it's time to build bigger church buildings or increase wages. When does it stop? Some religious ministers travel in private jets and limousines. Why? Where does the money come from? And why is it all in the name of God? Does God really ask for these material things, or is it the church leaders? We are all tired of being urged to donate more, and we deserve clarification. Perhaps it is time to take a closer look at tithing. What do you think?

Many wonder whether they need to tithe and how it relates to their spiritual journey. Let's begin by clarifying the premise. In Hebrew, "tithe" means a one-tenth portion of something. Traditionally, in the beginning tithing is believed to require giving at least one-tenth of the increase of one's annual earnings from that of the year before. Historically, the church used this contribution as a form of tax to support itself, though the church exercised more power in those days than it does today.

However now, most pastors will tell you that a tithe is the first 10 percent of your total income. THIS IS UNEXCEPTIBLE. If you follow them, THEN YOU ARE NOT FOLLOWING GOD'S WORD. However, if you follow YAHWEY in the Bible, His instructions differ. If God wants something from you, He will specify what and how much. You are free to act as you wish, but I choose to listen to YAHWEH rather than a pastor who wants a new car with my money.

Some pastors justify the 10 percent tithe with the story of Jericho:

"But all the silver, and gold, and vessels of brass and iron, are consecrated unto Yahweh. They shall come into the treasury of Yahweh" (Joshua 6:19, The Cepher).

These are things that come only from Jericho. As the story goes, the Israelites, with the help and guidance of Yahweh, destroyed ten towns before it was over. If Yahweh asked for just those things from one of the ten towns, doesn't that sound like He was asking for 10 percent of all of it from the ten towns? Many might agree with this logic. One out of ten would be one-tenth, or 10 percent. I suppose I might go along with that if only half of my brain were being used. But what changes if I use all my brain to think about this?

The problem, as I see it, is that the pastor's conclusion would be right if—and only if—each town had the exact same amount of gold, silver, bronze, and iron that Jericho possessed. Once we find that some of the other towns had more, the 10 percent theory collapses. So let me ask: Who is it that you follow religiously? Is it Yahweh or your religious leaders? I am not saying you must change your tithe. Yahweh will tell you what He wants from you. Just ask Him, and He will let you know. Also, the story of Jericho was a one-time event. In other words, the Israelites were not required to give the same amount of wealth week after week, year after year. Nowhere in the story of Jericho is there mention of a tithe.

The Bible does, however, tell us of an "annual tithe." See Deuteronomy 14:22–29 (KJV):

Thou shalt truly tithe all the increase of thy seed, that the field bringeth forth year by year. And thou shalt eat before the Lord thy God, in the place which he shall choose to place his name there, the tithe of thy corn, of thy wine, and of thine oil, and the firstlings of thy herds and of thy flocks; that thou mayest learn to fear the Lord thy God always. And if the way be too long for thee, so that thou art not able to carry it; or if the place be too far from thee, which the Lord thy God shall choose to set his name there when the Lord thy God hath blessed thee: Then shalt thou turn it into money, and bind up the money in thine hand, and shalt go unto the place which the Lord thy God shall choose: And thou shalt bestow that money for whatsoever thy soul lusteth after, for oxen, or for sheep, or for wine, or for strong drink, or for whatsoever thy soul desireth: and thou shalt eat there before the Lord thy God, and thou shalt rejoice, thou, and thine household. And the Levite that is within thy gates, thou shalt not forsake him; for he hath no part nor inheritance with thee.

Every three years, the "annual tithe" became the "third-year tithe":

At the end of three years, thou shalt bring forth all the tithe of thine increase the same year, and shalt lay it up within thy gates. And the Levite (because he hath no part nor inheritance with thee), and the stranger, and the fatherless, and the widow, which are within thy gates, shall come, and shall eat and be satisfied; that the Lord thy God may bless thee in all the work of thine hand which thou doest. (Deuteronomy 14:28–29, KJV)

I have been told many times that the 10 percent is a general rule of thumb. Do not misunderstand me—I am not against tithing or giving offerings.

That all sounds good and straightforward. However, we need to decide just what a tithe is. And then, just like that, it hit me: A tithe then, and still today, is a portion of our income. Now, if we tithe the way the Bible instructs, you might say, "But I have no corn, wine, or oil to give." Let us fast forward to what may be considered today's tithe. This is something I have concluded after studying how tithes were given in the past. Perhaps it is time we catch up with the times in which we live.

What might our tithe look like today? Since most of us have a job or a business, I am speaking of income. We must look at it from that perspective. Here is how it might work:

- You finish school and enter the job market.
- In your first year of work, your tithe would be zero dollars.
- In the second year, your tithe would be 10 percent of the increase between the first and second year.
- In the third year, your tithe would be 10 percent of the increase between the second and third year, and so on.

It is only in years of increase that you tithe (Deuteronomy 14:22–29, Cepher). If you lose your source of income, then that year your tithe would be zero.

Where do you take your tithe? As the Bible says, to the place God tells you. Most likely, that is the church you attend. If not, He will guide you elsewhere. Remember, the Church is the congregation, not the building—though you will most likely find the congregation in the building. The tithe is usually considered a once-a-year event.

The Bible does not specify when the tithe year ends. One might conclude it is after the harvest, or perhaps on the anniversary of when you began your job or business. I believe that one-tenth of your income is what pastors want, not what God requires, because it is not proven by scripture.

We tend to follow religious leaders because we believe they know more than us. The truth is, they gain their knowledge from the same book you have on your shelf. They, like us, are to abide by the laws of YAHWEH and preach what He has given in the Bible. There is little difference between a religious leader, a scholar, and a truly devout person. All we need to do is read scripture carefully and try to understand the circumstances in which it was originally written. Scholars and leaders can help us, but the responsibility to discern remains ours.

As you can see from the above quotes, it is acceptable to trade the tithe for money. When the tithe is too heavy to carry or transport, it is permissible to convert it into money. Fascinatingly, the King James Version states that once the tithe is delivered to the place where the Lord has established His name, the tithe can be converted into money. The Bible then adds: "And thou shalt bestow that money for whatsoever thy soul lusteth after, for oxen, sheep, wine, or strong drink" (Deuteronomy 14:26, KJV).

Now, for those who say God forbids drinking alcohol—you may want to read that last part again. It is also important to note that this tithe gathering was only a once-a-year event for the first two years. The third-year tithe was different. "At the end of every third year, you shall bring out the tithe of your produce of that year and store it up within your gates" (Deuteronomy 14:28, KJV). "And the Levite, because he has no portion nor inheritance with you, and the stranger and the fatherless and the widow come and eat and be satisfied, that the Lord your God may bless you in all the work of your hand which you do" (Deuteronomy 14:29, KJV).

Now that we know what a tithe is and where it goes, we must ask: What is the tithe used for? Yahweh wants His people to prosper and always do better.

In ancient times, this tithe gathering was a way to improve the quality of your herds. Suppose your tithe was two sheep. You could take those sheep to the place of the tithe and sell them, then use the money to buy a better-quality sheep. That one sheep would improve the future generations of your flock.

When the tithe was over, you were to take home whatever you bought and any leftover money. Yes, leftover money.

It's important to note that all of the older Bibles that were printed back in the 1500s, like the Geneva Bible, the Bishops Bible and also the King James Bible, have the word "increase" in Verse 22. WHO took the word increase OUT.

With all that said, and after searching through numerous Bibles, I have found something disturbing. I always thought that whichever Bible you read, each one had the same wording and context. But in recent decades, many newly printed Bibles no longer include the same words as those printed centuries ago. Although easier to read, they have omitted the most important word in Deuteronomy 14:22, which is *"increase."* God used the word *increase* in that verse to protect the poor. Man has removed it to his monetary advantage. What do you think about that?

Chapter 7
The Offering

The subject of offerings is different and can be controversial, particularly for those involved with churches. Some argue that tithing is no longer relevant in the modern era, leaving many to question its purpose. I am among those who have raised that very question.

Let me ask you a few questions:

1. Do you like having a place where you and your family can go to experience church together?
2. Do you appreciate it being warm when it's cold outside and cool when it's hot?
3. Do you like having a dry place when it rains?
4. Do you prefer a location with indoor restrooms?
5. Do you value someone leading and delivering sermons?

This list could go on and on. My point is that it costs something to maintain a church building and its grounds. While this may not fit the strict definition of an offering, it certainly helps keep the lights on and the doors open. Offerings serve as acts of worship, thanksgiving, commitment, and support for the needy, as seen in the Old Testament accounts of building the tabernacle and the New Testament teachings on generosity.

In Corinthians 9:7 (NIV), it emphasizes giving what you have decided in your heart to give, not reluctantly or under compulsion, because God love a cheerful giver.

Does an offering have to be money? I believe there are other ways of providing an offering. The building will need maintenance, and if there is a lawn, it must be cared for. Money is always easier to work with, but it is also the easiest way to get into trouble. We need to realize that an offering does not have to go through a church. You can give an offering through other channels as well. It does not need to be in the form of money. You can simply help someone with food, clothing, medicine, or money—in the name of YAHWEH. All this will suffice.

It is also not what YAHUSAH would want us to do. We need to help each other and watch each other's back. However, you must keep a clear head when helping others. There are those who will prey upon your emotions. Some people will take advantage of your kindness. Not that it is wrong to have emotions—we all tend to help others based on them—but you must make sure you are helping the right people. You need to know what the person truly needs before you reach out. You must understand what they lack or what needs have been unmet in order to help them.

So, if you are going to help those standing on a street corner, try to help them based on your knowledge of what they may need, not simply on your emotions. If their sign says, "NEED FOOD," then give them food, not money.

Have you ever noticed that the time for tithes and offerings is not far into the church service itself? I suppose that is as good a time as any. Get the collection out of the way so that the people can devote their attention to the sermon.

Offerings in Christianity

Offerings differ from tithes. Unlike tithes, which obligate a person to give a set amount, offerings are a matter of free will. You decide how much to give, and it is often believed that the more one gives, the more one receives. Think of offerings as seeds: The more seeds you sow, the more plants you may harvest.

In essence, the Old Testament is grounded in a system of sacrificial offerings performed by priests during rituals to atone for humanity's sins, particularly those of the Israelites. Offerings are abundant throughout the biblical text, symbolizing grace given to God and the restoration of a person's relationship with the Creator. This concept reaches its fulfillment in the New Testament with the crucifixion of Jesus, representing the ultimate sacrifice to restore humanity's connection to God. I will expand on this later in the chapter.

Some examples of Old Testament offerings include the following:

Burnt offering

The burnt offering was central to Israelite ritual, performed daily each morning and evening. It provided a deeply personal experience and was intended to leave a lasting impression on the worshipper:

> And he shall put his hand on the head of the burnt
> offering; and it shall be accepted for him to make atonement
> for him. And he shall kill the bullock before the Lord, and
> the priests, Aaron's sons, shall bring the blood and sprinkle

the blood round about the altar that is at the door of the tabernacle of the congregation. (Leviticus 1:4–5, KJV)

To atone for sin and receive God's acceptance, the worshipper would lay a hand on the animal's head. After the animal was slaughtered, it was understood to die on behalf of that person. Neither the priest nor the worshipper would eat the meat; it was completely consumed by fire. This was sacrifice in its purest form: the giving of an animal wholly to God.

Peace offering

The fellowship offering, also called the peace offering, was more than a sacrifice; it was a shared meal. A goat, sheep, or bull would be divided among the priests, the Lord, and the person offering it. Families, friends, and others could also participate. The act reminded the worshipper that communion and fellowship with God could be restored through the shedding of sacrificial blood.

Guilt offering

The restitution offering went beyond sacrifice and addressed the need for repair. The worshipper confessed guilt publicly and offered a blood sacrifice. In addition, they had to make full restitution and add 20 percent to the original fine, ensuring that the cost of sin was fully acknowledged. Leniency could encourage repeat offenses and set a dangerous precedent.

Principle of substitution

Levitical laws taught the Israelites that God accepted the blood of a substitute. While sacrifices were burdensome, they allowed sins to be forgiven without the sinner paying the penalty directly. Selecting an animal from the herd was often challenging, and the journey to Jerusalem could be difficult, particularly for those living far from the city. The physical, spiritual, and emotional demands of making a sacrifice were significant. Ultimately, the priest would perform the act of sacrifice by slitting the animal's throat.

Sin offering

The sin offering cleansed the individual of unintentional sins, allowed for forgiveness, and restored purity after defilement. The type of offering often depended on social status: a poor person might offer a dove or pigeon, a high priest might offer a bull, and a destitute individual could use fine flour. In all cases, the offering allowed people to atone for their sins. Leviticus references the sin offering repeatedly:

> And he shall bring his trespass offering unto the LORD
> for his sin which he hath sinned, a female from the flock,
> a lamb or a kid of the goats, for a sin offering; and the
> priest shall make an atonement for him concerning the sin.
> (Leviticus 5:6, KJV)

Chapter 8
Money

It sometimes seems as if our world revolves around money. Money, it appears, is the source of all troubles. So why would God the Father ensure that His Son, Yahusah, received the riches of a king? You say it was a king's treasure. What makes me believe that Yahusah was a wealthy man? Let us return to the period of His birth. The Magi from the eastern kingdoms came to view the newborn Son of God and brought treasures with them. That's right—the Bible states that they brought *treasures*, not gifts.

In the world of royalty, when a child deemed to be a future king is born, surrounding kingdoms send treasures to honor that child. They send treasures because money has always been a source of power, and power buys alliances. Moreover, no one likes to follow a poor man. That is why such children are bestowed with riches from the moment they are born. It is a way to show others that they hold higher status and are not equal in stature.

Here is a question that may sound contradictory to the statements above: Was Yahusah a rich man or a poor man? Why did He have so many followers if He was not wealthy? For the sake of fun, let me add the following verses. Yahusah was prophesied to be the Son of God, in the royal bloodline through His mother Mary from King David, and destined to become the King of Kings. That is the winning trifecta of power. The authority this child would one day hold terrified King Herod. That is why Herod sought to murder the newborn child. Not knowing His identity, he ordered his men to slaughter all newborn males under the age of two. Herod could not allow anyone to exist who might acquire the people's trust and loyalty.

There would have been no New Testament or Christianity if the angel had not told Joseph to pack his belongings and leave town. The major question now is whether we should think differently about YAHUSAH as if He was wealthy rather than destitute. When I discovered this, I realized it made no difference. He is still the same person I have always imagined Him to be. I find it fascinating that YAHUSAH never boasted about wealth or made people feel uncomfortable. It must have taken great self-control. I doubt I could have acted the same way. It takes a special kind of person to do that.

"And again, I say unto you, it is easier for a camel to pass through the eye of a needle than for a rich man to enter the kingdom of God" (Matthew 19:24, KJV).

Does this rule out the possibility of a wealthy person entering heaven? No, not at all. It means that, like your clothes, your money cannot go to heaven with you because it remains among the material things of Earth. Your spiritual being is the only thing that goes to heaven.

Remember, right before He was crucified, YAHUSAH gave away everything He had. Even He could not take anything with Him. To Him, money was worldly, and it could not help in His death. Another frequently misquoted verse is, "Money is the root of all evil" (1 Timothy 6:10, KJV). In truth, the verse says that "the love of" money is the root of all evil.

Does this imply that money itself is bad? If so, what about all the evil that existed before money? We have been taught that it is the love of money that corrupts, not money itself.

Even though we live in a different environment today than two thousand years ago, religious organizations still say they need more money. They always seem to have insufficient funds. I have attended churches of every kind—poor, wealthy, and those in between. One thing they all share in common is the time set aside for tithes and offerings. Members have been, and will continue to be, expected to give. It seems that human nature is to believe that donating more money to a religious organization improves one's chances of going to heaven. But giving more will not improve your chances whatsoever.

Most people work hard for their money to provide for their families. I have heard clergy say that working hard to improve one's status in life is fine—if you give God His due. What exactly is that part? Many struggle to make ends meet, yet they still contribute to the collection plate. Many enjoy donating, but if you look closely, many believe giving is expected even when it is not required.

I once attended a church with friends where the sermon was about people not donating enough. "Is buying a new car or taking that expensive vacation necessary?" "Can't you find it in your heart to do a bit more for Jesus, even though He gave up His life for you?" These were just two examples. It was an hour of hearing how we all needed to rethink our spending habits and possibly give Jesus a raise. That was the last time I visited that church. Clergy do not have the authority to pressure people to give more. I have seen the same tactics used on religious television shows. There seems to be a never-ending tug-of-war over how my money should be spent.

When I was younger, this plagued me for a long time. I had to figure out where my misunderstandings came from. I was shown something I had read many times before, which I now see as brilliant. I wondered how I had overlooked it. What made me feel at ease about whether I was giving my fair share?

Consider the Sermon on the Mount. Yahusah never had a collection plate passed around. Instead, He distributed enough fish and bread to feed thousands—many of whom did not belong to the same religious group. *Wow!* That showed me that money is not as important as we make it. Yes, we need money to live comfortably. Luxury is not a necessity, but it is not inherently bad. God blesses whom He wills. If you have wealth, it is not necessary to donate it all to the church.

When a person dies, God does not require that their money go directly into a church treasury. That is why there are wills, which allow the deceased to share it with whomever they wish. That is all I know. I do not know about the entire world, but I do know we all need money to survive and thrive—and so does the church. I still believe in tithes and offerings. But no matter how much money you have, you cannot buy your way into heaven. Remember, God has already explained what portion he expects from you. If you want to follow a newer Bible or follow that Paster that says you need to give until it hurts, that's on you. It will not give you a better chance to go to heaven. Think about it.

Chapter 9
The Sabbath

For a millennium, the church has been divided over the ongoing practice of the Sabbath. At the heart of the matter lies the day of the Sabbath, dividing people and the church alike. The debate is complex and has been argued for centuries. More to the point, this debate requires careful thought about the relationship between the biblical covenants, which compounds the problem further. Yet Christians agree that covenants are central to the Bible's narrative, even as they remain divided on the practice—primarily on the precision and instruction found in scripture.

During the early church, the apostles wrestled with the implications of Christ's work, particularly those that highlighted the errors of the Judaizers. Yet here we are today, still disagreeing over the word of Christ and the scriptures. These issues have transcended generations and persisted for millennia.

I wish to settle this debate in this chapter once and for all. When we read the following commandment in Exodus 20:8–11 (KJV):

> Remember the *Sabbath day*, and keep it holy. Six *days*
> shalt thou labor and do all thy work. But the *seventh day*
> *is the Sabbath of the Lord* thy *God:* in it thou shalt not do

any work, thou, nor thy son, nor thy daughter, nor thy manservant, nor thy maidservant, nor thy cattle, nor thy stranger that is within thy gates. For in six days the Lord made heaven and earth, the sea, and all that in them is, and rested the seventh day: Wherefore, the Lord blessed the Sabbath day, and hallowed it.

As we can see, Saturday is the seventh day of the week—the day God Himself selected as the day of rest. Later, through the events of history, Sunday became the day of worship and rest. Interestingly, Sunday was the first day of the week. Some claim that most Christians are going against the Sabbath commandment when they rest on the first day instead of the seventh. I have studied the matter at length, and I have a definite answer.

There is a whole recorded history on this subject. As I will show, Christians are following something instituted as a rule during the Roman Empire. However, those staying true to the Bible can safely state that Saturday is still unequivocally the Sabbath day.

It is often claimed that God instituted the Sabbath in Eden, due to the connection between creation and the Sabbath in the Exodus passage above. The verse in Genesis 2:3 (KJV) foreshadows a future Sabbath law. However, it must be noted that no biblical record of the Sabbath exists prior to the departure of the children of Israel from Egypt. Yes, you read that correctly: There is no record that the Sabbath was practiced from Adam to Moses.

It arose at a special point in Abrahamic history. Reading the Bible makes it clear that YAHWEH first initiated the Sabbath for the Israelites. We see this in Exodus 31:12–17 (Jerusalem Bible):

Yahweh said this to Moses, "Speak to the sons of Israel and say, You must keep my Sabbaths carefully, because the Sabbath is a sign between myself and you from generation to generation to show that it is I, Yahweh who sanctified you. YOU must keep the Sabbath, then; it is to be held sacred by you. The man who profanes it must be put to death; whoever does any work on that day shall be outlawed from his people. Work is to be done for six days, but the seventh day must be a day of complete rest, consecrated to Yahweh. Whoever does any work on the Sabbath day must be put to death. The sons of Israel are to keep the Sabbath, observing it from generation to generation: this is a lasting covenant. Between myself and the sons of Israel the Sabbath is a sign forever, since in six days Yahweh made the heavens and the earth, but on the seventh day He rested and drew breath."

In Deuteronomy 5:12 (KJV), Moses reiterates the Ten Commandments to the Israelites. In verses 12–14, he explains why the Israelites are to observe the Sabbath. Then Deuteronomy 5:15 (NKJV) states:

And remember that you were slaves in the land of Egypt, and the Lord your God brought you out from there by a mighty hand and by an outstretched arm. Therefore, the Lord your God commanded you to keep the Sabbath day.

The intent of God in this verse was purposeful. It was not simply to remind the Israelites of creation, but rather to help them remember their slavery roots and the deliverance provided by Yahweh. There are particular requirements for keeping the Sabbath, which include the following:

- "Let no man go out of his place on the seventh day" (Exodus 16:29).

- "You shall kindle no fire throughout your dwellings on the Sabbath day" (Exodus 35:3).

- "In it you shall do no work: you, nor your son, nor your daughter, nor your male servant, nor your female servant, nor your ox, nor your donkey, nor any of your cattle, nor your stranger who is within your gates, that your male servant and your female servant may rest as well as you" (Deuteronomy 5:14).

- "Whoever does any work on the Sabbath day, he shall surely be put to death" (Exodus 31:15), with similar language in Numbers 15:36.

When we examine the New Testament, the passages show us important aspects:

- When Jesus Christ appears in His resurrected form, the day mentioned is the first day of the week (John 20:19–26; Luke 24:1, 13, 15; Mark 16:9; Matthew 28:1).

- When the Sabbath is mentioned from Acts through Revelation, the context is Jewish evangelism, with the synagogue as the backdrop. Once Paul announces that he will visit the Gentiles, the Sabbath is not mentioned again.

Rather than basing the argument on adherence to the Sabbath, the New Testament goes in the opposite direction. No one should allow themselves to be shamed into following special requirements about food, drink, festivals, new moons, or Sabbath days. To do so is to give more authority to a religious leader than to Christ Himself (Colossians 2:16).

Additionally, the New Testament shows that no obligation exists for believers to keep the Sabbath. The idea of a Christian Sabbath on Sunday is therefore unscriptural. This concept is addressed again in Romans 14:5–6 (Cepher):

> One man esteems one day above another: another esteems every day alike. Let every man be fully persuaded in his own mind. He that regards the day regards it unto Yahuah; and he that regards not the day, to Yahuah he does not regard it.

And Galatians 4:9–11 (Revised Standard) further states:

> But now that you have come to know God, or rather to be known by God, how can you turn back again to the weak and beggarly elemental spirits, whose slaves you want to be once more? You observe days, and months and seasons and years! I am afraid I have labored over you in vain.

The main question remains: How did Sunday come to be the Sabbath in the first place? This is an area of immense confusion among modern Christians and likely reflects the ignorance of the history of religion in the Roman Empire.

The Jews lived in relative harmony across the Roman Empire in the first century. They were protected by Rome and allowed to practice their religion freely. Things remained stable until the Judaea rebellion, which resulted in major changes in how the Jews practiced their faith. As the first century dawned, Jewish communities spread rapidly across the Mediterranean, from Judaea into Greece, Egypt, and Syria. These communities were often unpopular due to their differences in faith, and so they preferred to live in close-knit groups to protect themselves and their religion.

By the second century, Jews were inhabitants of Rome itself. Rulers such as Augustus and Julius Caesar had enacted laws protecting Jews and allowing them to practice freely. Synagogues were categorized as "colleges" to work around Roman laws forbidding secret societies. Jews also paid annual taxes for the maintenance of temples. This created a stable environment in which Christians could spread and thrive within the Roman Empire.

Christians began their week with Sunday, owing it to the Lord's Day. This trend was influenced by both the pagan planetary week and the Jewish week. After the fourth century, the Christian week became an official institution in the Roman Empire. Emperor Constantine declared Sunday a day of rest for judges, artisans, and other workers.

In 321 AD, Constantine decreed:

"On the venerable day of the Sun let the magistrates and people residing in cities rest, and let all workshops be closed" (*Codex Justinianus* lib. 3, title 12, 3; trans. Philip Schaff, *History of the Christian Church*, vol. 3, p. 380, note 1).

More laws regarding Sunday were enacted to ensure that Christians would be less involved in labor on the Lord's Day. One notable law from 370 CE prohibited tax collectors from visiting Christians on Sundays. This official recognition gave Christians an advantage that Jews did not possess.

Christians could abide by governmental rules without directly entangling themselves with the state, while Jews faced greater difficulty since the rest of the Roman Empire continued working during their Sabbath.

Constantine's actions can also be evaluated in light of his earlier policies. He favored the Christian demographic in his territories and enacted pro-Christian measures throughout his reign. Even his father, Constantius, pursued policies that favored Christians and avoided harsh treatment.

Constantine rejected anti-Christian policies that had been in force during his time. He quickly passed laws enabling Christian churches and their members to regain property confiscated during earlier persecutions. Over time, he adopted a distinctly pro-Christian stance, favoring laws that placed Christians in positions of influence. History makes it clear that Constantine was a proud patron of Christianity, paving the way for its soaring popularity. His patronage was tied to the politics of the region as well. In contrast to the continual persecution of Christians in the eastern bloc of his empire, Constantine's support was welcomed when he extended his rule there.

The eastern bloc became his new focus, with Constantinople (modern-day Istanbul) as its capital. While in Rome, he enacted laws favoring worship on Sundays. He replicated these laws for his Christian brethren, granting them a day of worship.

This begs the question: Did he change the day of rest deliberately? As far as history is concerned, it seems far from the case. As I mentioned earlier, Christians were highly likely to worship on Sundays a hundred and fifty years before Constantine's arrival. However, his decision did much to further worship on Sundays rather than on the Sabbath. Beyond that, the newly converted Christian community found it more convenient to visit the church on Sunday instead of Saturday. This resulted in a wide spread of Christianity, rising to become a popular religion in the region. Thus, it seems Constantine made this change himself rather than through the papacy. The papacy was not yet established; it grew later from the office of bishop, continuing to prevail in Rome alone. As a result, we realize that Constantine made a significant and monumental change in the history of Christianity. It is clear that he was a man of the people and put them front and center.

Apart from the Christians, the pagan temples under his rule were free to carry out their religious proceedings with enthusiasm and zeal. These temples were also allowed to keep their endowments and treasures. The Roman emperor created a liberal religious ecosystem in his empire. We can say that Constantine was doing what any good ruler should do for his people. Pagans still constituted the majority of the empire at the time, and they enjoyed religious freedom just the same. Christians worshiped on Sunday, which coincidentally was an important day for the sun-worship cult as well. Later, pagan places of worship came under Christian control, and some of their annual festivals came to have pagan roots.

We can conclude, then, that Constantine did not alter the day of the Sabbath. He established Sunday as the day of rest for the people of the Roman Empire. It is not difficult to predict that Emperor Constantine made this decision. We can reasonably assume that it did not arise out of dislike for the growing Christian population within a thriving Roman Empire, but rather to adopt what Christians had already practiced for more than two centuries before him.

Jewish Christians observed the Sabbath, yet they would meet at day's end to convene on Saturday evening. The Gospels speak of women visiting the empty tomb. The famous Roman emperor Constantine decreed that Christians would not keep the Sabbath. They would keep only Sunday, the first day of the week, hailing it as the "venerable day of the sun." The Christians saw this decision as a day on which Jesus Christ rose from the dead and the Holy Spirit came to the apostles. This practice was old, dating back to AD 115, when Christians would meet for worship. When Constantine reinforced this during his reign, more Christians began to observe Sunday as the day of rest rather than the Sabbath. By the second century (as historical writings confirm), it was common to celebrate the Eucharist on a corporate day of worship—the first day of the week.

Having said all that, I can safely say that I would rather follow God than an earthbound ruler. This makes more sense to me than anything else. I have shown that worship on Sunday has no theistic roots whatsoever. Its origins are purely man-made.

YAHUSAH is the "Lord of the Sabbath" (Matthew 12:8, Modern Language Bible). He is God incarnate and truly decided the meaning of the Sabbath since he created it. Once, the Pharisees criticized Jesus Christ for healing someone on the Sabbath. Jesus was quick to point out that they should not think twice about pulling a sheep out of a pit on the Sabbath. As he rightly said, "The Sabbath was made for man, not man for the Sabbath" (Mark 2:27, KJV). It was perfectly acceptable to break the rules of the Sabbath. I will clarify this point further below. Jesus further said that men were more important—as was their salvation—than Sabbath rules. The core principle behind the Sabbath was that man was to rest and relieve himself of all labors.

God provided the law to the Israelites to encourage them to love others (Mark 12:30–31, Living Bible). He did not prohibit doing good for others or oneself on this day. The Pharisees felt that God had created this day so that they might subjugate him. Jesus clarified that God had presented the Sabbath as a gift to the people he had created (Mark 2:27).

This brings me to the final point of the chapter. It sums up the discussion about the ever-raging debate over Saturday or Sunday as the Sabbath day. It is not as difficult as people and churches make it out to be. People often quote a verse from Romans 14 as the final word on the debate. Well, there is an issue with that. On the face of it, the famed verse in Romans 14 provides ample reason to keep the Sabbath on a day of one's choosing. Many people follow it as well, because it is the word of the Lord.

Again, the appropriate verse is as follows: "One person esteems one day above another; another esteems every day alike. Let each be fully convinced in his own mind. He who observes the day observes it to YAHWEH; and he who does not observe the day, to YAHWEH he does not observe it. He who eats, eats to YAHWEH, for he gives YAHWEH thanks; and he who does not eat, to YAHWEH he does not eat, and gives YAHWEH thanks" (Romans 14:5, The Cepher).

People often quote this verse as an indication that the day of the Sabbath depends on the people of the Lord. However, I would like to clarify this further.

The Sabbath was created by ELOHIYM on the seventh day of Creation. Yet I cannot find anything in the Bible—or anywhere else—that unequivocally overrides the word of ELOHIYM. As far as I am concerned, no one has the authority to override the word of ELOHIYM. I usually call this "verse-a-sizing," because it is a great verse at face value. Most people look at the verse and confidently say that it alone gives us the authority to decide a suitable day for the Sabbath.

That is not the case. To understand the verse in its entirety, it is important to read the whole of Romans. That way, one can grasp the context and the historical backdrop behind it. Let me clear the air by showing what was taking place in history at this point.

Paul was sending a letter to the Romans. He was busy proselytizing the Romans, who were pagans and Gentiles for the most part. In his attempt to convert them to devout Christians, he tried to be flexible and give them leeway in their practices. According to Paul, the Romans were free to eat any kind of meat. Whether they were vegetarian or otherwise, it did not matter. He was building a bridge with them. His aim was to befriend them and treat them with kindness. As a friend, it was counterproductive to pick an argument—especially about their theology and existing customs.

As a result, he did not begin his proselytizing by advising against the consumption of pigs. To me, that was the right approach. If you invite someone to your belief system, it makes sense to be kind first. One cannot start with an argument. Also, the Roman Empire was vast, so proselytizing was a major undertaking for Paul.

So, we have this yin-and-yang situation. If you read the Bible, you see Christians, pagans, and Jews. Moreso, Gentiles appear in the scriptures as well. The more you read Romans, the more you find that Paul tried to create common ground with the pagans of the empire. He was attempting to connect with them personally. In doing so, he mentioned the flexibility of the Sabbath. For instance, Roman pagans had different holidays. Due to religious variances, their holidays differed from one group to another.

Thus, when Paul approached the Romans to bring the good news, he did it in his own way. One thing to note here is that Yahusah was born a Jew and died a Jew.

Let's turn to the New Testament. People often allege that it provides a fresh set of commandments for us to follow. That is not the case. Nowhere did Jesus Christ state that the previous commandments were to be discarded. He did, however, simplify them so the people could understand and follow them.

Yahusah observed the Sabbath as well. He broke Sabbath convention only in special cases—emergencies or situations where healing was needed—so His intentions were noble. Jesus made a strong point about breaking Sabbath ritual. As I mentioned before, He contended that if an animal fell into a ravine, you could not let it die. That would make no sense. You would save the animal, even if it was the Sabbath.

Interestingly, when the Sabbath was introduced, people did not have clocks or wristwatches. As a result, they needed a time frame for reference. The Jews would begin the Sabbath at sundown on Friday and end it at sundown on Saturday. I have no issue with this practice.

What I take issue with is the fact that I still do not see any authoritative body declaring that the Sabbath was changed from Saturday to Sunday. It was made for rest. Sunday was mandated for rest by Emperor Constantine. Sunday is called the Lord's Day because Yahusah rose from the dead on that day. This may be unknown to many.

Christ died on a Friday but did not rise that day. He could have risen on Saturday—anytime from morning until night—but He chose not to rise on the Sabbath. He rose on Sunday. In one way, we can allege that Yahusah did follow the Sabbath, even in His resurrection. It is important to note that the Sabbath was given to all mankind in the first story of Creation.

As far as the Lord's Day is concerned, the Council of Nicaea was involved. They claimed that YAHUSAH rose on a Sunday. Therefore, it should be called the Lord's Day. Yet when we read that event, it does not reference changing the Sabbath.

All I am proposing is that we need to follow the rules. I cannot find anything in scripture that says otherwise. Where did God say that the

Sabbath was changed to Sunday? I am willing to keep an open mind if someone can point that out to me. It is not in the Old Testament.

As a result, I see no reason for anyone to claim that the Sabbath is on Sunday or any other day. On whose authority was this claim made? As I said, the Roman verses describe a historical event. They were simply referring to the different holidays pagans observed. Pagans were free to do as they preferred. Do you see where I am going with this? The Bible was referring to a historical event during Paul's time.

The Lord decided a day for His people to follow. Man, on the other hand, decided to create a day of rest to his own liking. In conclusion, I reiterate the point: To the best of my knowledge, ELOHIYM created the Sabbath for His people to rest, and that day of the week is Saturday. Emperor Constantine made a law that allowed Christians in Rome to rest on Sunday, the first day of the week. Remember that Monday is the first workday of the week for most people. YAHUSAH said that every day is a good day to worship.

Chapter 10
A Little About Yahusah

As you have already noticed, I refer to the one you call Jesus as YAHUSAH. This is because a name is a name, and there is no reason to translate it into a different language. If you were to go to France and someone asked you your name in French, what would you tell them? Would you give them the name you were given at birth, or would you give them your name translated into French? No—you would give them your birth name since that is who you are. Not all names can be translated into other languages. The name *Jesus* is almost universally acknowledged, regardless of religious beliefs. YAHUSAH was the original Hebrew birth name of Jesus. I will use both names interchangeably throughout this book.

Since Jesus and his followers were all Jews, they were given Hebrew names, even though they spoke Aramaic. The "J" sound used to pronounce Jesus's name does not exist in Hebrew or Aramaic, indicating that he was known by a different name among his contemporaries. Hence, most scholars believe that the Christian Messiah's name was YAHUSAH, a very common Jewish name during Jesus's lifetime. Archaeologists have discovered the name engraved into seventy-one burial caverns in Israel, all dating from the time when the historical Jesus lived. The letter "J" was not invented until around the fifteenth or sixteenth century. Therefore, every word starting with J—such as Jesus, Joseph, Jerusalem, and others written in the Bible—did not originally begin with J.

With that being said, who decided to change YAHUSAH to the Hispanic name Jesus, and tell everybody that it was actually an English translation?

How many of you believe that Jesus was a Christian? I am sure most of you reading this have faith in Jesus Christ as a Christian himself. However, let me break it down. Jesus was a Jew. He was born in Galilee, a Jewish region, to a Jewish mother. His circle of friends, associates, colleagues, and disciples were all Jews. He attended Jewish community worship in synagogues regularly. He preached from Jewish texts. He celebrated Jewish festivals. He went on pilgrimages to Jerusalem's Jewish Temple, where priests guarded him. He was born a Jew. He lived, and died, as a Jew.

There is no indication in the Gospels that Jesus was anything other than a Jew. The idea of a "new religion" is foreign to the Gospel text and to Paul. That concept emerges only later. To declare that he was a Jew is a truism. It is simply presenting a notion so self-evident that one wonders why it needs to be stated at all. Yet it is necessary, because we all know what happens later in the story when Christianity evolves into something distinct from Judaism. As a result, Jesus is sometimes viewed in hindsight as something other than a Jew—as the founder of Christianity.

Yahusah started a movement to reform Jewish laws and traditions that were burdening the people. He also made it possible for those who worshiped other gods to find refuge and salvation in his Father. The Jewish priests were adding new laws and traditions that enriched themselves while impoverishing the people. Something had to be done, so Jesus began a nonviolent revolt.

One distorted belief is that Joseph and Mary were poor. In reality, Joseph was a carpenter or possibly a laborer. Mary and Joseph were in Bethlehem to pay taxes. The reason Jesus was born in a stable was that Bethlehem was overcrowded with others also there to pay taxes. None of the inns had room for them; therefore, they were fortunate to find shelter in a stable. Shortly after Jesus was born, Mary, Joseph, and Jesus were able to find lodging in a house. The Bible tells us that when Jesus was born, shepherds came to see him first (Matthew 2). Later, in Luke 2, the Magi came bearing treasures of gold, frankincense, and myrrh. They found Jesus in that house and gave him those treasures. Why, then, are we made to believe that Jesus's family was poor? As I mentioned earlier, people will only follow someone rich and/or intelligent. Additionally, no one would follow a person who was not influential.

Jesus's intelligence came from who he was, not from a formal education. How is that possible? The simple answer is that he was born with it. He was born with an intellectual mind. Think about who taught Sir Isaac Newton the laws of gravity and motion. Who taught Tesla about alternating current? Who taught Einstein the theory of relativity? Great thinkers and inventors are God-gifted and naturally possess extraordinary minds. Thank God for them, or else we would still be living in caves.

We have grown up listening to stories of our ancestors. Kings of old were extravagant. When an heir to a king's throne was born, neighboring kings sent treasures to the royal child. The gifts and wealth the infant heir received were more than enough for him to live a wealthy life. Why mention ancient kings here? To make a stark distinction between the lifestyles of Jesus and other kings. The important insight is that what set Jesus apart from kings and wealthy men was his humility. He never flaunted his wealth or misused his power for personal gain. He knew he was to become a king—not on Earth, but the King of Kings. Yet his simplicity and down-to-earth nature never changed.

I cannot imagine a person who knew he would inherit a kingdom in heaven being so disciplined. Imagine how difficult it is to have all the world's riches and yet not use them for personal benefit. Could we, as ordinary people, overlook wealth? Obviously not. We would buy the biggest house, the fastest car, the most expensive clothes. We would upgrade our lifestyle. But Jesus did not even consider doing this. Despite having riches, he remained disciplined.

Let us now learn more interesting facts about Jesus. He was born a demigod. His father was a God, but his mother was mortal. For Jesus to become fully divine, the mortal part of him had to die. This is one reason Jesus had to die. Many followers of modern Christianity emphasize his struggles before crucifixion. Yet the only way Jesus could attain the status of God and be on the same level as his Father was for the mortal part of him to die.

There are seven billion people in this world, and everyone has free will. People will always believe what they want. I do not intend to change your mind about Jesus. I simply want to state accurate facts and explain the adversities he endured to become our Savior and God.

Another important aspect I have researched is how Jesus got his name. In Matthew 1:23 (Jerusalem Bible), it states that he will be named

Emmanuel. In Luke 2:21 (Cepher), it says he would be called Yahusah. I honestly do not care if you call him Jesus or Yahusah. That is for you to decide; however, for me, His name will always be YAHUSAH. Your name is your true identity. For instance, my first name is Cletus. People have asked if I had "Clete" as a nickname, and I told them, "No, my name is Cletus."

In seventh grade, during French class, the teacher told me, "There is no name for Cletus in French. You can substitute it with Claud." I was not pleased. I like my name. I always thought that if I went to France and someone asked my name, I would not give them a French version. I would give them my real name. That is who I am. Therefore, I believe in calling people by the name they were born with—the name their parents, friends, and relatives used. Jesus was called Yahusah by those around him. Hence, his name is Yahusah, and I think we should call him by his real name.

We think of God as the only one. Muslims have faith in Allah, their one and only God. Hindus have numerous gods, and they pray to each by name. Many of our traditions also come from the Torah. The Torah is a vast scroll with profound insight into what God tells us to do and what He wants from us.

According to Yahusah, if we want to go to heaven, we must first go through him to reach the Father God. One interpretation is that whenever someone is sick, hurt, or in pain, we should ask Yahusah for help. In the Bible, YAHUSAH possessed the power of healing. There is no specific mention of God healing, but this does not mean that God is not capable of healing. Having said that, YAHUSAH did cure people. Therefore, when we or someone around us is sick, I believe, we should pray to Yahusah, call out his name, and he will send healing. What do you think?

Another interesting aspect of Jesus's life is what we call the sixteen lost years. The New Testament begins with his birth and continues until he is thirteen. Everything after that is skipped until he reappears at twenty-nine. What happened during those sixteen years? They are not mentioned in the Bible. It is said that Jesus visited the kingdoms that had sent him treasures, thanking them for their gifts. There are also stories of him studying religions such as Buddhism and Hinduism.

To conclude the chapter, I would say, if you do not understand something I have explained, please take a second look.

Chapter 11
Back to "In the Beginning"

When I first started writing this book, I thought I knew exactly how it was going to end. I believed I had the content and flow planned out. It seemed like it would be a piece of cake to write because I had a plan and knew how to execute it. But it turns out that people change—and so do plans.

Initially, this book was supposed to end with me talking about all that I had been shown throughout this shared experience. However, the closer I came to the last chapter, the more I realized that the most important part of this book was in the first chapter, not the last, as is common in books. As I checked off each chapter from my imaginary checklist, I felt that every next chapter was more important than the one before.

My focus throughout this book was to explain, to the best of my ability, what I had been told and shown. I realized that the chapters I had written were essentially the way I received them. During the first few chapters, I began to sense that something was missing—that something was amiss and needed further discussion. By the time chapters 9 and 10 rolled around, it became clear to me that the end of this book was not going to be what I had anticipated. Writing this book has certainly been a learning experience.

Something about my first chapter was different from the rest. I had written something I was very passionate about; however, I will now backtrack a bit and discuss some of the ideas I was supposed to mention there. I hope I can do justice to all my findings.

Elohiym (Gods) never said that the Earth was flat. Nowhere in the Bible does Elohiym—or any God, including Yahweh—say that Earth was flat. Remember, the people of the time believed that the Earth was flat.

It is important to remember that the first books in our Holy Bible were taken from the Jewish Torah. By the time Jesus came into the world, those words had already been written. The Old Testament was a partial collection of books from the Torah, which was written for the Israelites.

Additionally, the Old Testament does not contain everything written in the Torah. The portions included in the Bible give us some insight into the bloodline from which Jesus came. From Adam to Jesus's birth, this bloodline was kept intact through his mother, Mary. Redundantly, please recall that Jesus was a Jew, born to a Jewish mother. I know this may be information some find hard to digest.

The Bible says that in the beginning, Elohiym created the heavens and the Earth. When this verse was revealed, the people of that time knew nothing about the universe or other planets. Given the information and technology they had, I believe it is safe to say that I, too, would have concluded that the Earth was flat. But we now know the truth: the Earth is a sphere. The puzzle pieces were always in the box, but it took science to help us put them together correctly.

Because of the way Genesis, Chapter 1, verse 1 was written, they could just as easily have believed that the Earth was a planet, and that it was round. There was no need to reinterpret the verse; the unchanged verse is sufficient to give us the correct explanation. This is why I believe it would be better to teach that, in the beginning, the Earth ELOHIYM created was, in fact, a planet. Why is this important—at least for me personally? If we understood that the Earth was a round planet, it would be easier to grasp how there was more than one human race. When one reads about the occurrences of the sixth day of Creation, this fact helps us understand how other races were placed around the planet.

We were all created equal. No race was given superiority over another. How do I back up this claim? In a very simple way. Have you noticed that all races share the same biological structure? We all have the same body parts—skin, bones, legs, arms, head, feet, and so on. The major biological difference is the amount of pigment in the skin of each race. There are differences among races in terms of culture and faith, but those are not factors that make anyone less human.

If we, as people, were different—and the gods had made us different— we would never have been able to have children together, nor would we have been able to exchange body parts such as hearts, lungs, kidneys, or parts of the liver. Think about it. We are all interchangeable. We can give and still survive.

It appears that what makes us different has nothing to do with biology. It has nothing to do with the way we are made. Instead, our differences are based on nurture and how we were reared. As it says, in the beginning we were all created in the likeness and image of our creator gods (ELOHIYM). The gods, or ELOHIYM, are equal in stature and rank. Therefore, we are all created to be equal in stature and rank. This is some of the information I was given to share with you.

Now, with that out of the way, let's come to the real reason for this chapter. Let us travel back to chapter 2 of Genesis and the story of Adam. The Bible suggests that Adam's purpose was to till the land and make it cultivable. It is important to understand that Adam was created for a special task, and there was no plan for him to have a mate as the animals did. It should also be noted that animals were not created equal to humans.

Some animals are herbivores, while others are carnivores. Some are a combination of both. Among the millions of creatures that have walked, swum, and flown on this planet, only a few can naturally mate. Most of the time, two different species cannot mate and produce offspring with the characteristics of both parents. Such combinations are possible only in a science lab.

Returning to the topic: did you notice that ELOHIYM created both male and female humans and told them to be fruitful and multiply in the first story of Creation, on the sixth day? Did you also notice that there was no mention of a Tree of Life or a Tree of the Knowledge of Good and Evil in that first story? Most likely, there was a reason for this.

As you know, Adam was created outside the garden and later placed inside the garden in the eastern part of Eden. Adam was not created differently, but it seems he may have been created for a special reason. He was not created with the knowledge of good and evil. That knowledge would be given when the time was right. The right time would be decided by YAHWEH, who would then allow Adam to eat the fruit from the Tree of Knowledge of Good and Evil and from the Tree of Life.

This is where we lose some connection between the two stories. It appears that the people of the first story of Creation were created with the knowledge of good and evil. During the time that the ELOHIYM rested on the seventh day (the Sabbath), these people were left on their own to use this knowledge. Some used it; others did not. Even though they had this knowledge, they still fell victim to evil. They knew, but they did not know how to use it properly. It was not until after the seventh day that YAHWEH

ELOHIYM saw the amount of evil in the world and reasoned that something else needed to be done.

This is when the second story of Creation begins. According to the Bible, Adam was created to till the soil, but perhaps there was another purpose. Maybe this was sidelined after evil convinced Eve and Adam to disobey.

One scenario I have been enlightened with is that the Lord God trusted Adam to do as he was told until the time he would be mature enough to fight evil. At that time, the Lord God would allow Adam to eat the fruit from the Tree of Knowledge of Good and Evil and from the Tree of Life. Adam would live in the garden (Paradise) and help all who came to learn and understand good and evil. However, things went sideways.

The plan was that, had things worked out as YAHWEH intended, Adam would be alive today, living in the garden and sharing with all people the knowledge of good and evil. Still being young, Adam and Eve were not mature enough to realize the importance of their situation. This is the case with many young people today as well.

The garden was a protected area, and evil could not enter unless someone allowed it. This is where the serpent came in. The serpent had no pact with the Lord God about the laws of the two trees in the center of the garden. Carrying the seed of evil, the serpent told Eve that she would not die but that her eyes would be opened, making her like the gods, with knowledge of good and evil.

This is how evil works: through deception and lies. Once you let it into your mind, driving it out is not easy. Throughout the Old Testament, there are stories of how evil tricked others in similar ways. In the New Testament, Satan (evil) challenged Jesus to leave the Lord God. This demonstrates how even Yahusah who was such an important figure, was challenged by evil. We, as ordinary humans, are obviously more prone to fall for evil's traps.

I now look at the Bible with a whole new perspective. The more I read, the more I learn about the knowledge of good and evil. Years ago, while driving to work and listening to a radio station, the hosts asked their listeners what they considered impossible questions. One was "What is the purpose of life?"

They thought this question was impossible because of the lack of knowledge surrounding it. Once you have the relevant knowledge, your path becomes clear. The meaning behind the question is: What is the one purpose all life forms have in common? Luckily, I had a forty-minute drive, and it took about thirty minutes for them to answer. Their answer was that the purpose of life is to reproduce. Without reproduction, there is only extinction.

"How true!" I exclaimed. Yet the more I thought about it, the more I felt their answer was incomplete. Over the years, that day's answer has bothered me. After much research and many conversations, I have finally come up with what I believe is the rest of the answer. This is my personal opinion, and I do not wish to push it on anyone.

Here is how it goes: "The purpose of all life is to reproduce. Without reproduction, there is only extinction. The word *reproduction* means different things to different people. Some believe it has only one meaning: to produce offspring. But reproduction also includes reproducing moral traits in our youth. It is to instill love, compassion, and understanding. It is to reproduce knowledge by teaching the young about good and evil. It is also about getting along with others, regardless of race, gender, creed, culture, religion, social standing, or financial situation."

We need to teach our young to be good neighbors and friends. We need to teach them to let the Lord God do the judging. We need to teach them to be good brothers, sisters, parents, grandparents, relatives. We need to teach them to be good human beings. Why? Because if we forget to reproduce knowledge, compassion, and love, these characteristics will become extinct.

What does this have to do with "in the beginning"? In the beginning, the first people were created with the knowledge of good and evil. Only some passed this knowledge down to their children. Others did not, and the knowledge became extinct in later generations. This is the point the Bible is trying to help us with: passing down the knowledge of good and evil. Without it, later generations destroy themselves in their evil ways.

Where did all this start? During Creation, Lucifer was cast out of heaven and down to Earth by the Lord (Luke 10:18, KJV). Then, on the sixth day of Creation, ELOHIYM created the first people. They were told to multiply and conquer the Earth. The Earth in this case meant this planet. They would have to do that to make it their home and keep the evil one from controlling it.

Good and evil are powerful forces. What makes them powerful? In the case of good, it is humans who commit to it. The way to end evil would be if all humans came together and attempted to end it. That is the only way.

On the other hand, how does evil get its power? Every time something goes wrong in our lives, we tend to blame God. How often have you heard someone say, "God, how could you let this happen to me?" or "God, this is all your fault"?

Every time we blame God for what has gone wrong, we give power to evil. It is time we teach ourselves and our families where the true blame belongs. Evil is what puts obstacles in our path and denies us what we deserve. Evil uses the old tactic of divide and conquer.

It is evil that causes rifts in our lives and then gets people to blame God, making evil more powerful and widespread. Remember, in the beginning, Eve was given a choice to obey God's command. She questioned it by entertaining the seed of doubt that evil placed in her mind. That doubt led to Adam and Eve's fall from grace.

It was evil that also caused the events that followed. Do you remember the story of Jesus in the desert? Satan tried to make a deal with him: Satan would give Jesus's power over all the people on this planet if only Jesus would bow down to him. By doing so, Jesus would be accepting evil and would become the Lord of Evil on this planet. But he would lose his place in heaven next to the right hand of Father God. He would also lose all the power that came with the position he was intended to hold. Jesus was blessed with the knowledge of good and evil; therefore, he knew that no one could ever trust evil.

Thank you, Lord God, for rearing Jesus correctly and giving him the knowledge of good and evil. If there is one thing we should pray for, let us pray that the Lord God will help us share our knowledge of the difference between good and evil with our children. There is a little more to say when it comes to bad and evil—specifically, how to distinguish between them. Not everything that is bad is evil. However, everything that is evil is bad.

This is where the knowledge of good and evil comes in. I will not tell you that learning this knowledge is going to be difficult, but at the same time, it will not be easy either. Perhaps it is better to say that it might be simpler if we just allow it. If you open your mind to it and commit, you will have a better chance of receiving the crucial knowledge between the two. This will be a lifelong learning experience.

This is one of the reasons we have a church. We have church so we can share our experiences with others, have fellowship, and perhaps come up with better solutions to the problems we each face. Remember that the church is not a building. The church is the congregation—the people. So pray, and pray with unity. So live, and live with unity.

No one has all the answers to the hurdles and problems that will befall us. We need answers and solutions to the events and problems that evil has caused. We must greatly reduce the power we give to evil each day. We need to start placing the blame on evil where it belongs and praise God for all the good things in our lives.

Chapter 12
Something Further to Think About

One more subject I have been meaning to talk about—something I admit I have been guilty of on occasion—is understanding the difference between good and evil. To put this in perspective, I would like to share a story about a young lady.

She seemed to have a wonderful life. She had ambitions, dreams, and a career, but none could withstand the test of fate. One night, the life she had built for herself came crashing down. She lost everything she had worked so hard for, leading her to ask the same question mentioned in the previous chapter. As I noted earlier, many of us have asked at some point in our lives: "God, how could you let this happen to me?"

After a series of unfortunate circumstances, her happy marriage could no longer stand the test of time. Newly divorced, with two young children and an ex who could not remember to pay child support on time, she struggled to make ends meet. Each month was a battle to rein in her feelings of despair. Again, she asked, "God, how could this happen to me? I have been good, haven't I?"

Then, one day, things took a turn for the worse. In the afternoon, her boss called a group of employees into her office and told them she had bad news. Business was too slow to keep all of them employed, and she would have to let some go. Clearly, the group she had called in was the unfortunate bunch. Yet again, the young lady's life plummeted into darkness. "Oh, God, how can this happen to me?" she cried out in desperation.

Just when she thought all hope was lost, something strange happened. About two hours after that meeting, another employee came to her boss and announced that they had decided to retire earlier than planned—six months sooner. The boss called the young lady back into her office and gave her the great news: she could keep her job for now. Overwhelmed by what had just happened, the young lady broke down in tears. *What a day*, she thought. One moment she was in despair, and the next moment things were looking up.

She finished the day at work, then went home to feed her children and remind them how much she loved them. She decided to take a long, hot bath. Afterward, she put the children to bed, tucked them under the covers, and told them stories of faraway lands and brave queens. Once they were asleep, she sat in an armchair with a cup of coffee in hand, reflecting on the day's events and pondering the design of her luck. After the good news and the soothing bath, she felt revived.

Her reverie was interrupted by the ringing of her phone. It was her friend, inviting her to attend the birthday party of a mutual friend. At first, she declined, but after some persuading, she relented. She called her babysitter and convinced her to return, on the condition that she would not stay out too late.

Since the divorce, she had not been able to do much of anything, mostly because she could not afford to. But tonight seemed like a good night to celebrate—and celebrate she did. At the party, she encountered a few people who brought back unpleasant memories. After a couple of drinks, however, she no longer minded their presence. Hours of nonstop partying passed before she remembered her promise to the babysitter. "Does anyone know what time it is?" she asked aloud. No one heard her over the loud music. Panicked, she told her friends she was late and had to leave immediately.

"Oh, God, how could this happen to me?" she exclaimed once again, frustrated and overwhelmed. By now, she had developed a pattern: complain, recover, complain again. She was not concerned with self-evaluation in these circumstances. Life was hard, and she believed that was enough to consider herself a victim.

As she made her way to her car, someone asked, "Are you sure you're okay to drive? I can give you a lift." She dismissed the offer and headed toward her car for the trip home.

Somewhere on the interstate, the effects of alcohol began to challenge her ability to drive. Late-night driving is difficult for many, and a car ahead of her abruptly changed lanes. The swerve caught her off guard. She did not realize she had been traveling at 110 mph. At that speed, there was little time to make the right decision. She slammed on the brakes, causing her car to swerve and collide with the concrete median. Just before impact, she realized she had forgotten to fasten her seatbelt. That realization became reality when she was thrown through the passenger window during the collision.

The impact was horrendous. The car that had changed lanes became entangled with hers, and it took time for both vehicles to come to a halt.

Her parents were notified and arrived at the hospital moments before she was brought in by ambulance. The EMTs wasted no time getting her into the emergency room. Her parents caught only a glimpse of her as she was wheeled past—barely recognizable. One of them cried out, "Oh, God, how could you let this happen to our child?"

Her injuries were extensive. She lost her right leg; her face was mostly torn off; she had internal injuries along with multiple broken bones and contusions. Yet somehow, she was still alive.

What does the young lady's story have to do with good and evil? To understand it better, we need to examine her life. Since no one likes to pick apart their own life, we will use her experience as an example. We know little about her, but I imagine her life was going well until something happened in her marriage. Some people feel that as their marriage ages, it seems to lose something—like a pair of shoes that no longer feel the same as when they were new. So, ironically, they think it is time to get a new pair.

But marriage is much different than worn shoes. A marriage itself does not get old; people and shoes get old. What happened to her marriage? I will not dive into all the problems because I already know the answer. Somewhere along the way, evil planted a seed. If that seed is allowed to grow, it will most likely destroy the marriage. You can be assured that God did not destroy this or any other marriage. Those who say marriage is a fifty-fifty relationship do not understand marriage. Marriage is "one hundred percent" from both sides.

The day the young lady found out she was losing her job was not God's fault. After she learned her job was spared, did she thank God? I doubt it. That night at the party, it was not God who made her drink too much. God even tried to get her home safely by sending someone willing to give her a ride. It was evil that tried to destroy her life. God kept her alive and guided the surgeons who put her back together. Some people seem to know what God has in store for them during their lives. The rest seem to discover it only when their lives are nearly over, as they become wiser.

This is just one story. There are millions more like it. Something bad happens, and instinctively, we blame God. We curse, mourn, and cry for His attention, yet somehow, He is the one we blame first when things go wrong. Somehow, it is always God who is at fault, who supposedly did not do His job right or watch over us in our most critical time. We do this because it is easier to place blame on others than on ourselves. No one wants to take responsibility for their failures, mistakes, or the spiral into despair.

Like you, I have sat through sermons where the preacher tells us that God has a plan for us. During those sermons, I often asked myself, *Wait just a minute! Are you trying to tell me that God also plans that bad things are going to happen to us?* God doesn't plan bad things for us – evil does. When I hear that, I refuse the concept altogether. Not my God! Over the years, I have thought about this notion and realized there is no source for it. It is time we put more thought into this.

Why is it that when something bad happens, we tend to place the blame on God? Who should we blame for the bad and evil in our lives? Is it us? We tend not to want to blame ourselves. We did not plan for these things to happen. Who did?

Anytime I encounter a problem beyond my capabilities, I know I will find the answer in prayer. I learned years ago about good and evil—the praised and the damned. They were the center points of my existence over the years. Let's not forget the difference between good, evil and bad. God is good, yet sometimes he will put obstacles in our paths. Sometimes these are to make us stronger and sometimes they are placed there to move us off that path to another.

Some of you may not realize this, but there is a war raging between good and evil. Remember, it started when ELOHIYM cast Lucifer and his followers out of heaven and down to Earth. This war has been going on since the days of Creation.

As with every war, there are two sides. The first team is God and His followers—"Team Good." The other team is Satan and his followers—"Team Evil."

When we are born, we are born into Team Good. We have a spirit, and our spirit is our power. This war is about power. Whichever team ends up with the most power wins everything, including the fate of mankind. As we grow older, we start to be seduced by Team Evil. We are taught in church and school, by parents and grandparents, to be good. When we allow evil to persuade us to commit immorality, we give away some of our power. If we do not check ourselves in time, we will be consumed by immorality, giving evil all our power. Often, we do not even realize it is happening. Evil forces are so clever that sometimes they do not even need to act—humans let their doubts consume them.

First, God does not plan for bad things to happen. Evil does. Second, God does not hurt or kill people. Evil does. God does not help you make bad decisions. Evil does. God only does good. Yet why does evil seem to have so much power over us?

Tactics. It is that simple. Using tactics can get people to do things, especially when the victims do not know what tactic is being used. This tactic has been around since the beginning of time. What is this powerful tactic? As mentioned before, it is divide and conquer. It is the most well-used tactic in wartime.

Why? Because it works—and Satan uses it best. By planting a seed, even smaller than a mustard seed, one can divide people into factions. It is that easy. The thought that one group is better, smarter, or better looking than another can create huge waves within a population.

Why do people let others plant doubts in their heads? If we are fortunate, most of us start with one head, two eyes, a nose, a mouth, two ears, a body with two arms, two hands with fingers, a torso with two legs, two knees, and two feet with toes. Basically, everything everyone else has in common.

Do you care if your neighbor has brown, green, blue, or hazel eyes? Does it matter if they are taller, shorter, or the same height? Does it matter if they are stronger or weaker? This is only the short list. If you think about it, why does skin color matter so much to so many? Is it really the color of skin, or is it something else? The gods who created us were equal. They created us in their likeness and image. Thus, if the gods who created us are equal, then we should consider ourselves equal. I have thought long and hard on this subject, and I could be wrong. Think about what I have been shown, then decide for yourselves. Yes, that may take another prayer or two, plus a little wait time.

What was it that got Lucifer and nearly one-third of the angels who followed him cast out of heaven? The answer that came to me was *attitude*. Isn't it our attitude that causes most, if not all, of our controversies?

Ask yourself: How many times have I blamed God for something bad that happened to me? How many times have I thanked God when something good happened? No one wants to be blamed for something bad or for something they did not do. Do you?

Here is the twist. Most of us say we want to be on Team Good. If so, we need to work harder to be members of Team Good. Given a choice, most people would want to be part of Team Good.

Remember years ago, when you and your friends decided to play a sport? Two captains would take turns picking players until the teams were complete. There was always one player who would say, "Pick me, pick me!"

The captains could either ignore that person or choose them. But they did not pick players because someone wanted to be chosen. They picked based on ability and attitude.

I am afraid this is also how you will be picked for Team Good or Team Evil. You do not get to decide which team you want to be on. That will be decided based on what you do and how you do it. I have had to rethink many of my choices, and maybe some of you feel the same way. It is simple. Every day, I must ask myself: *Am I a candidate for Team Good? Do I need to check my attitude?* If you are true to yourself, you will know the answer. Contemplate your thoughts about this.

Conclusion

As I stated before, I was not sure where this book was taking me when I began writing it. Then, suddenly, the direction was right before me. It was not until I was proof reading it that my mental visualization of the puzzle became clearer. The knowledge I was seeking was, once again, already there before my eyes.

Have you ever heard the saying, "Can't see the forest for the trees"? I seemed to get caught up in looking for that certain tree from time to time—even to this day. I found myself regressing when I thought I was making headway. Prayers, prayers, and more prayers. Then, waiting for an answer. As always, it came to me in the middle of the night.

I realized the problem was simple: I could not see the whole puzzle because I kept spending too much time looking at the pieces. That was when it hit me. I was consumed by my preconceived information and knowledge about the Bible. Preconceived information and knowledge are like old habits—and old habits are hard to break. As this book evolved, it became clear to me that it is more about those preconceived ideas we learned earlier in life. They are not complete truths and they make it more difficult to see and understand the puzzle.

While instructing other pilots to become instructor pilots, every now and then one would say he had just done something out of an old habit.

Then he would add, "Old habits are hard to break." I had to agree, because I too had experienced the challenge of learning to fly different helicopters. I realized that breaking old habits can be difficult, even nearly impossible. So, what needs to be done? I told him, instead of spending time trying to break old habits, spend that time learning the new habits you need for the new aircraft. Keep the old habits for when you fly the helicopters you have already been trained in.

There will be those who tell you not to read or discuss this book. They will insist that every interpretation of the Bible is the same now as it was when it was written. If that were true, let me share something with you.

There is something interesting about the story of Jesus and the adulteress woman whom he saved from being stoned to death. Many church leaders preached that the woman he saved was Mary Magdalene. It was not until 1963 that the Church realized there was no evidence in the Bible proving that Mary Magdalene was, in fact, the woman he saved. She could quite possibly have been just another person in the crowd. Many who died before 1963 died believing Mary Magdalene was the adulteress.

As for the outcome of the puzzle introduced in this book, my interpretation is that it is not be a two-dimensional picture. It is a four-dimensional picture, which includes the future.

There are those who can think outside the box, and those who cannot. As for me, I had to step outside the box and look carefully back into it. If I mentally place myself high above this planet, I can see the oceans, the mountains, and the fact that the planet is round. You may have to step outside of your comfortable box to fully comprehend this book.

Before you reread this book, consider the following old saying: "It is easier to fool people than to convince people that they have been fooled" (Mark Twain). Don't be fooled.

Now you have the encouragement needed to help with your interpretations of the Bible and its true message. Prayers will answer your questions and allow you to become closer to God. Amen.

References

The Cepher Bible. Cepher Publishing Group, 2014.

The Guideposts Parallel Bible King James Version, Modern Language Bible, Living Bible, Revised Standard Version. Guideposts, 1973.

The Holy Bible King James Version. Barnes & Noble Edition, 2012.

The Holy Bible King James Version. Christian Art Publishers, RSA, 2019.

The Holy Bible New King James Version. Thomas Nelson Inc., 1982.

The Holy Bible, Revised Standard Version, Second Edition. Thomas Nelson Inc., 1952–1971.

The Jerusalem Bible edited by Alexander Jones. Doubleday & Company, 1966.

The Net Bible Reader's Edition. Biblical Studies Press, Version 6r 715, 1996–2006. www.bible.org.

About the Author

Please know that I may not fit the definition of an author or storyteller as some of you may imagine. I am an armed helicopter instructor pilot who fought during the Vietnam War and retired in 2001 after thirty-two years of service. I am simply here to give you, I hope, a better understanding of the Bible as it has been shown to me. I am just a regular man who asked God if there was anything I could do for Him—especially after realizing how much He has done for me over the years.

Growing up, I engaged in religion as much as any average Christian. There was an acceptance of religious knowledge, but I was far from understanding its precious nuances. Still, a few near-death experiences and years of self-reflection compelled me to study the Bible as a stand-alone book, without carrying the religious baggage of my early years. Anyone willing to see the Bible as more than a religious guide will, I hope, find my efforts and research illuminating and helpful.

First, I noticed something in recent years that can be very misleading—something I call *verse-a-sizing*. It refers to people who know the Bible but use certain verses selectively, telling a story without including the entire chapter. These individuals either do not understand or misrepresent the context of those verses. In most cases, this leads them to preach a twisted, incorrect, or misleading story.

Second, asking questions about the Bible is controversial and often frowned upon. It is not considered fitting or normal to question divine words at all. Yet I am not questioning the words themselves—I am questioning their usage. As a result, conversations can become stilted, uncomfortable, or even aggressive. People often deflect, steering the discussion away from the topic at hand so subtly that one hardly notices. One might think the debate is still on the relevant subject, but in reality, it has shifted elsewhere—a sly trick.

Then there are those who take the Bible literally, and those who preach against taking it literally. Which is correct? There are many layers and underlying messages that must be studied carefully. Some interpret it literally because it suits their needs. Others use the Bible to drive their agendas, editing it according to their preferences and views. Throughout history, the Bible has been edited to fit the opinions of those in power— religious scholars, kings, and others. It depends upon their beliefs and perspectives. They edit the Bible as they see fit, often without portraying the true message or accurate stories.

Why did I receive this undertaking? That is the question I am sure you have now. As you read in this book, I explained my near-death experiences. Then, one day, I realized that perhaps I should thank The Lord who had been watching over me during those times.

In prayer, I simply said, "My Lord, thank you for all you have done to keep me alive. You have truly blessed my life, and for that, I ask you if there is anything you need me to do for you. Please let me know what I can do for you. Amen."

I had no idea what to expect. About five or six months later, I found myself searching for answers in the Bible. What I found was shown to me. What I was shown and told, was believable and understandble—and then I was told to share it with you. I hope you might agree with me, that there needs to be only one Bible for all Christians.